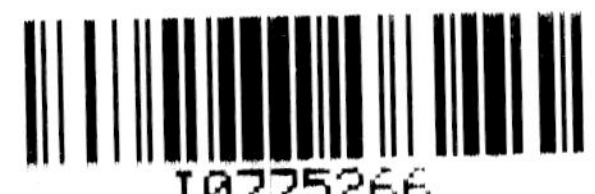

COLORING BOOK

PET'S FASHION

Shirley Simmer

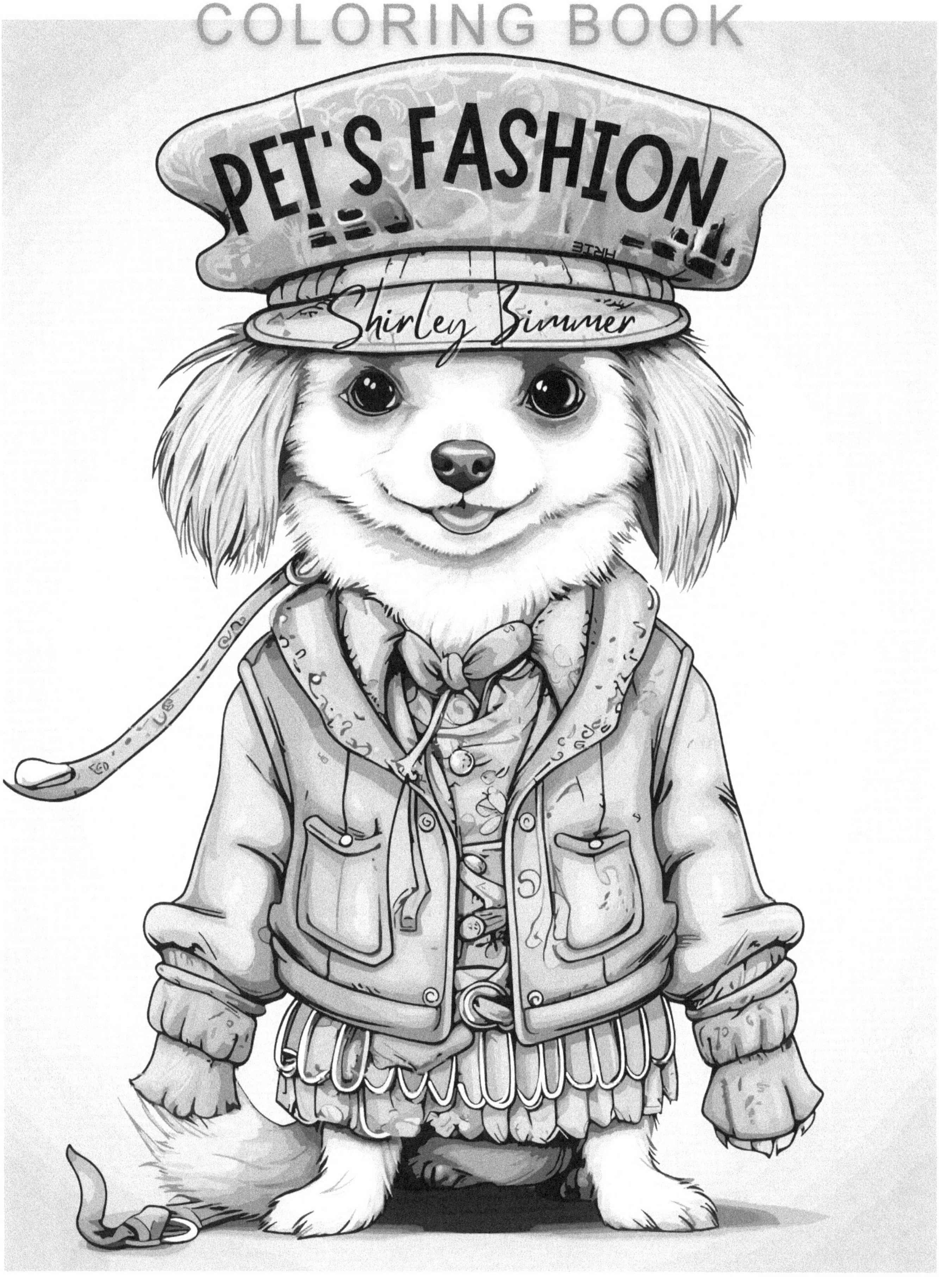

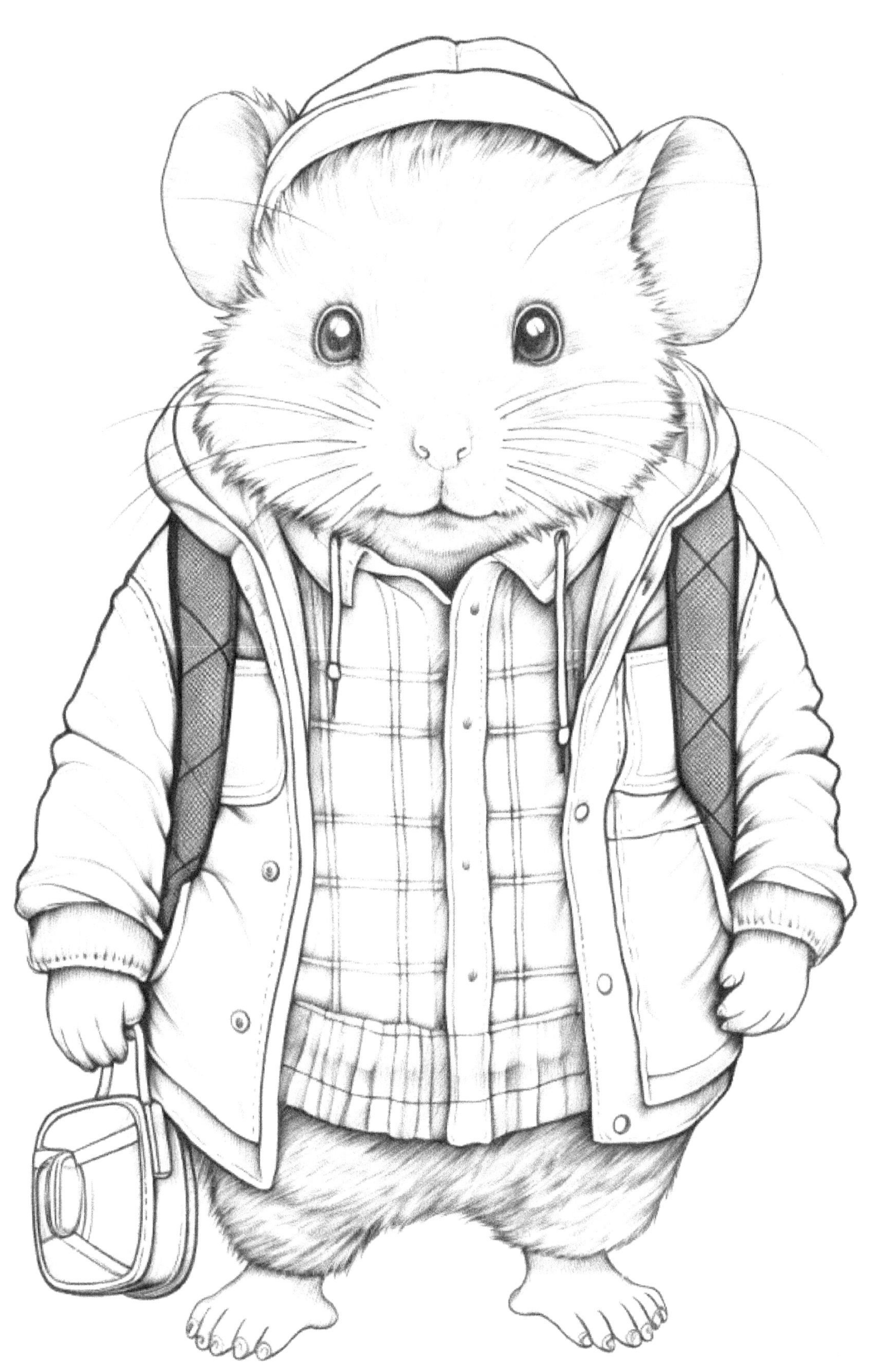

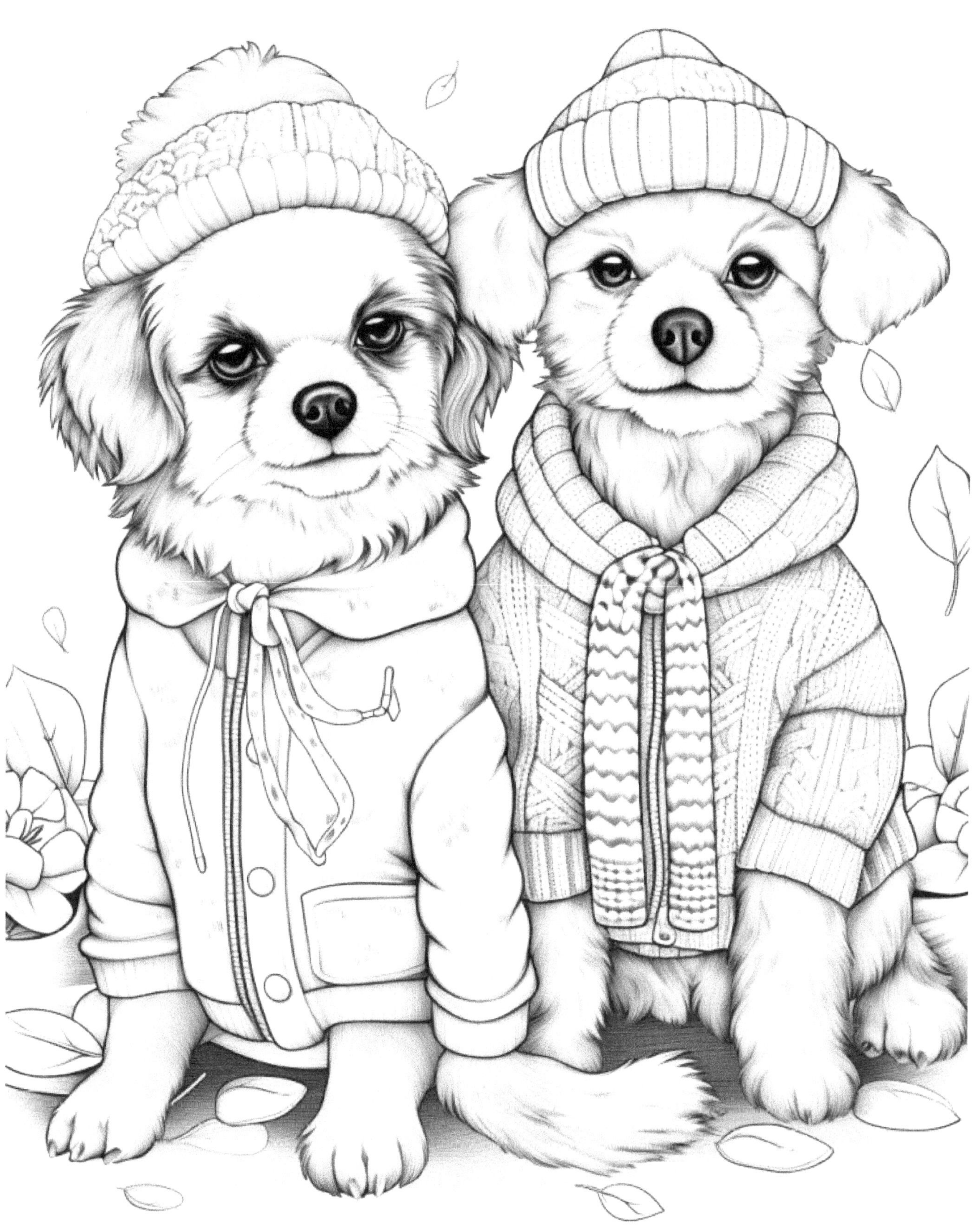

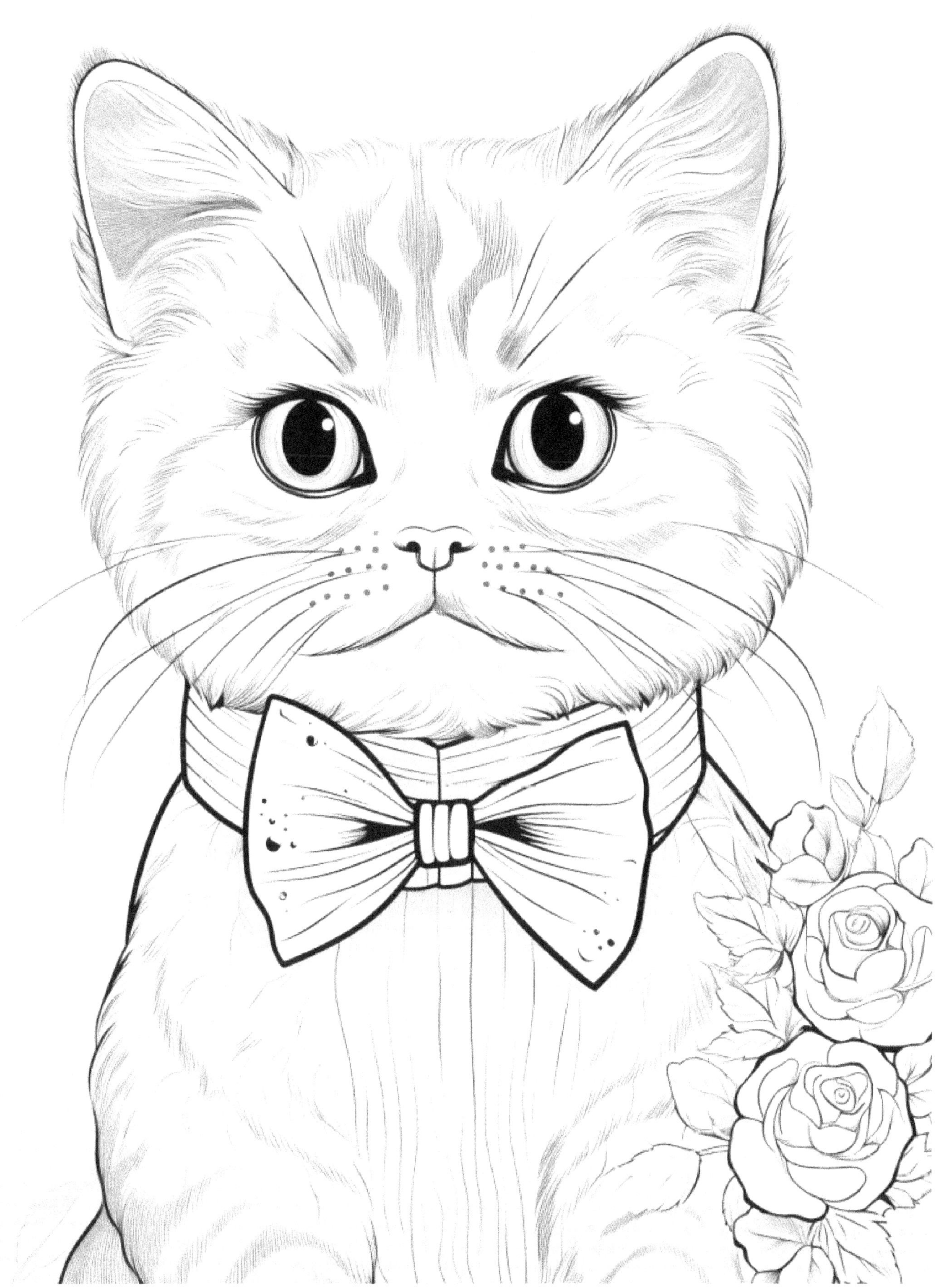

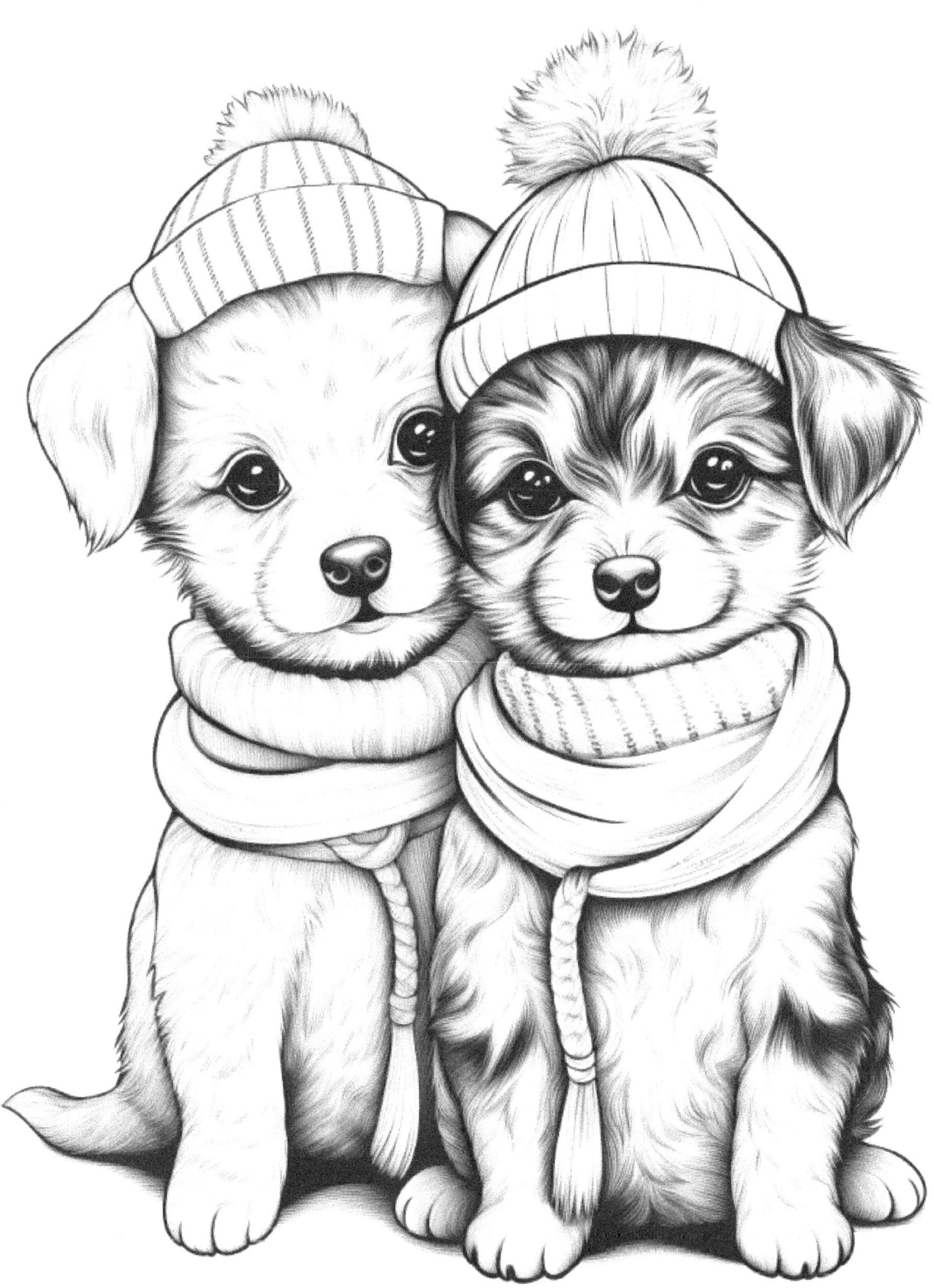

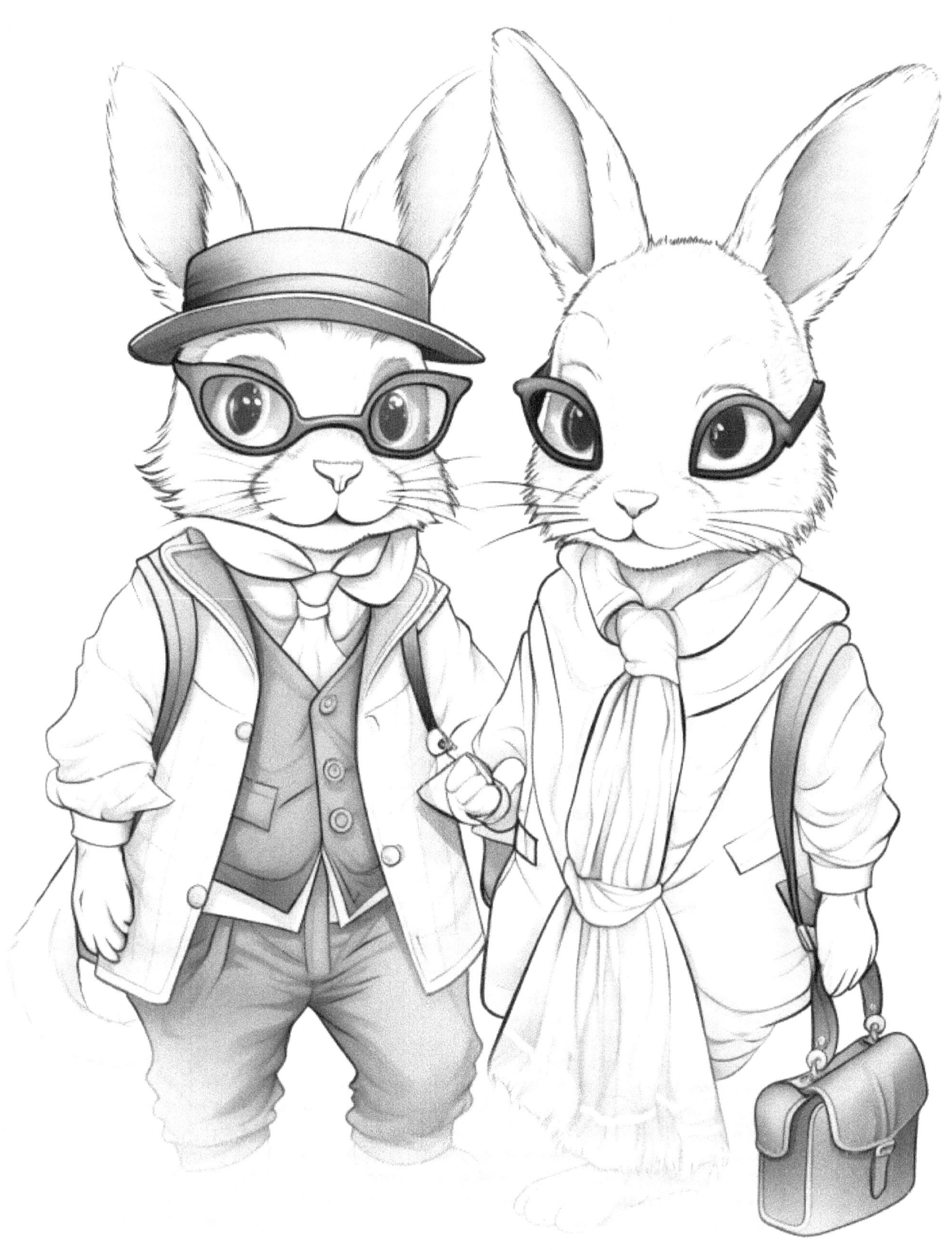

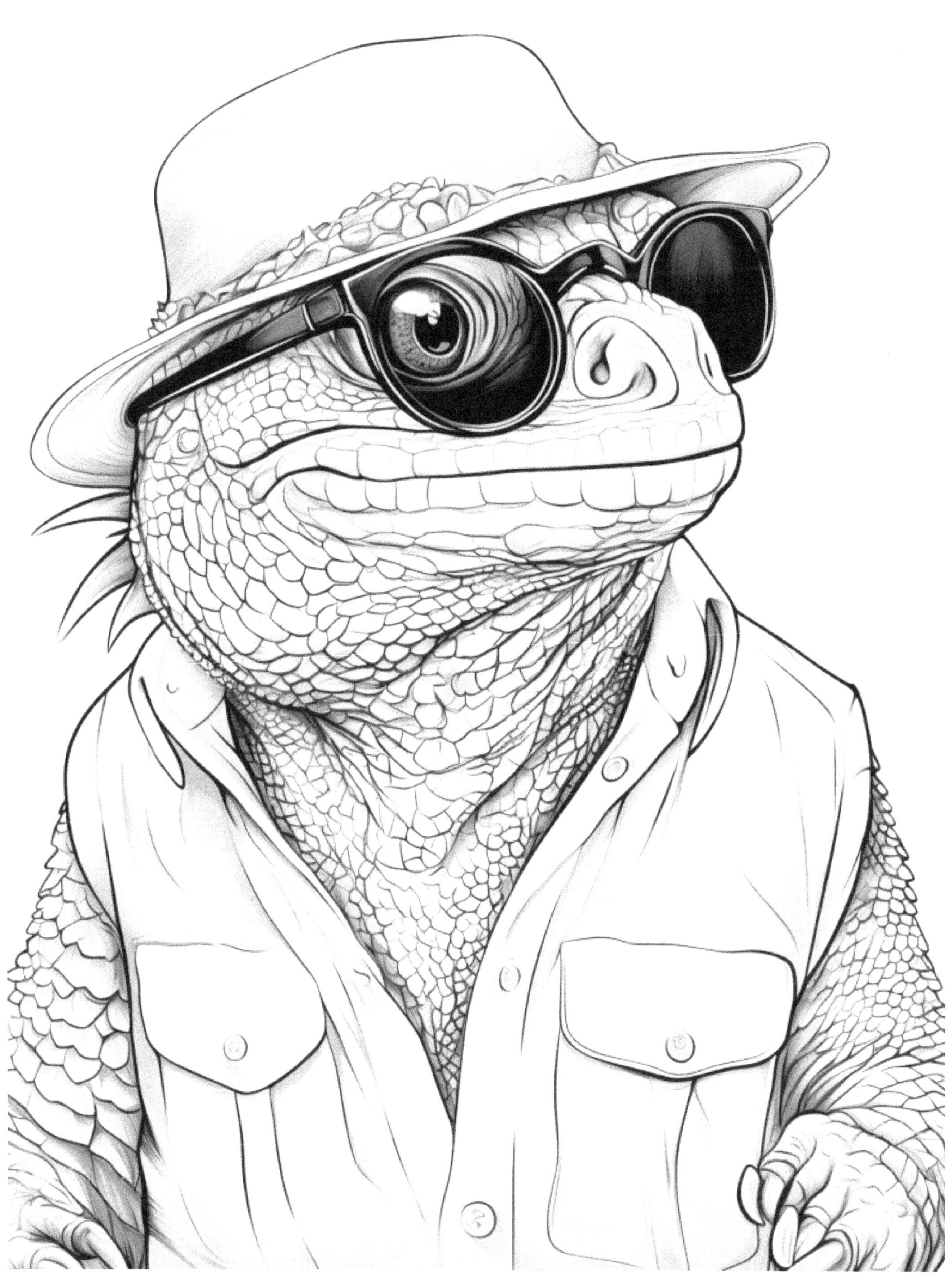

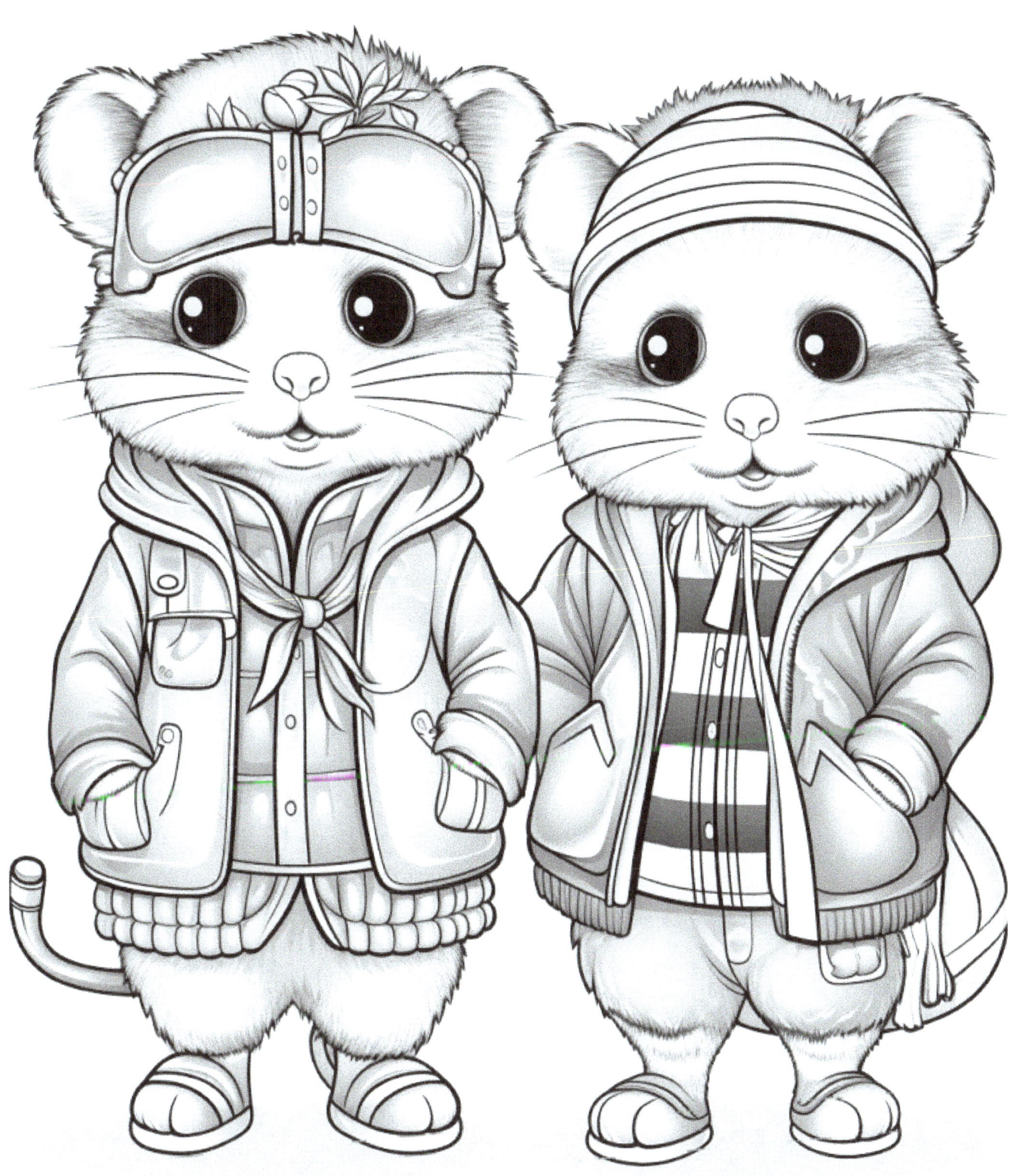

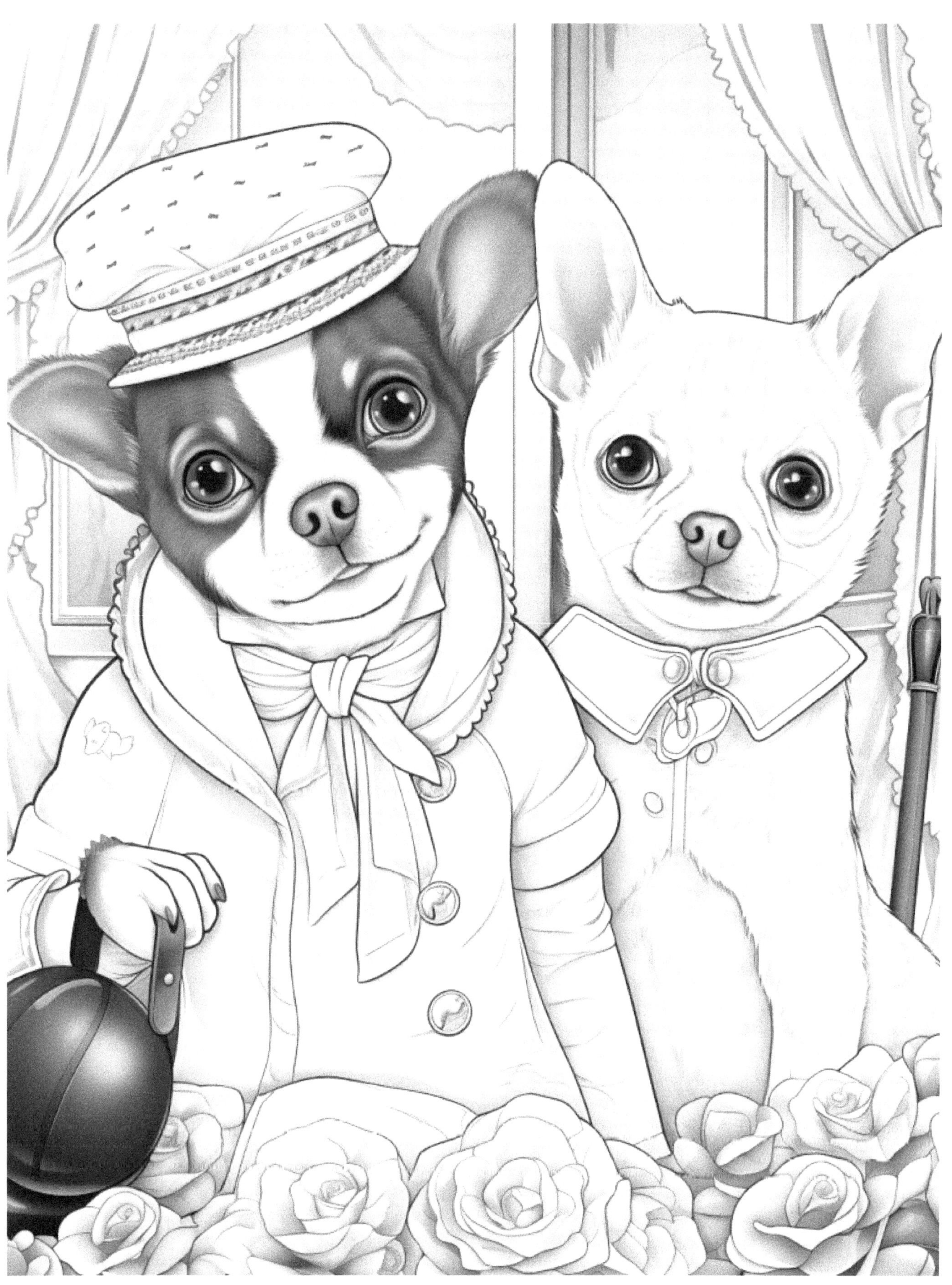

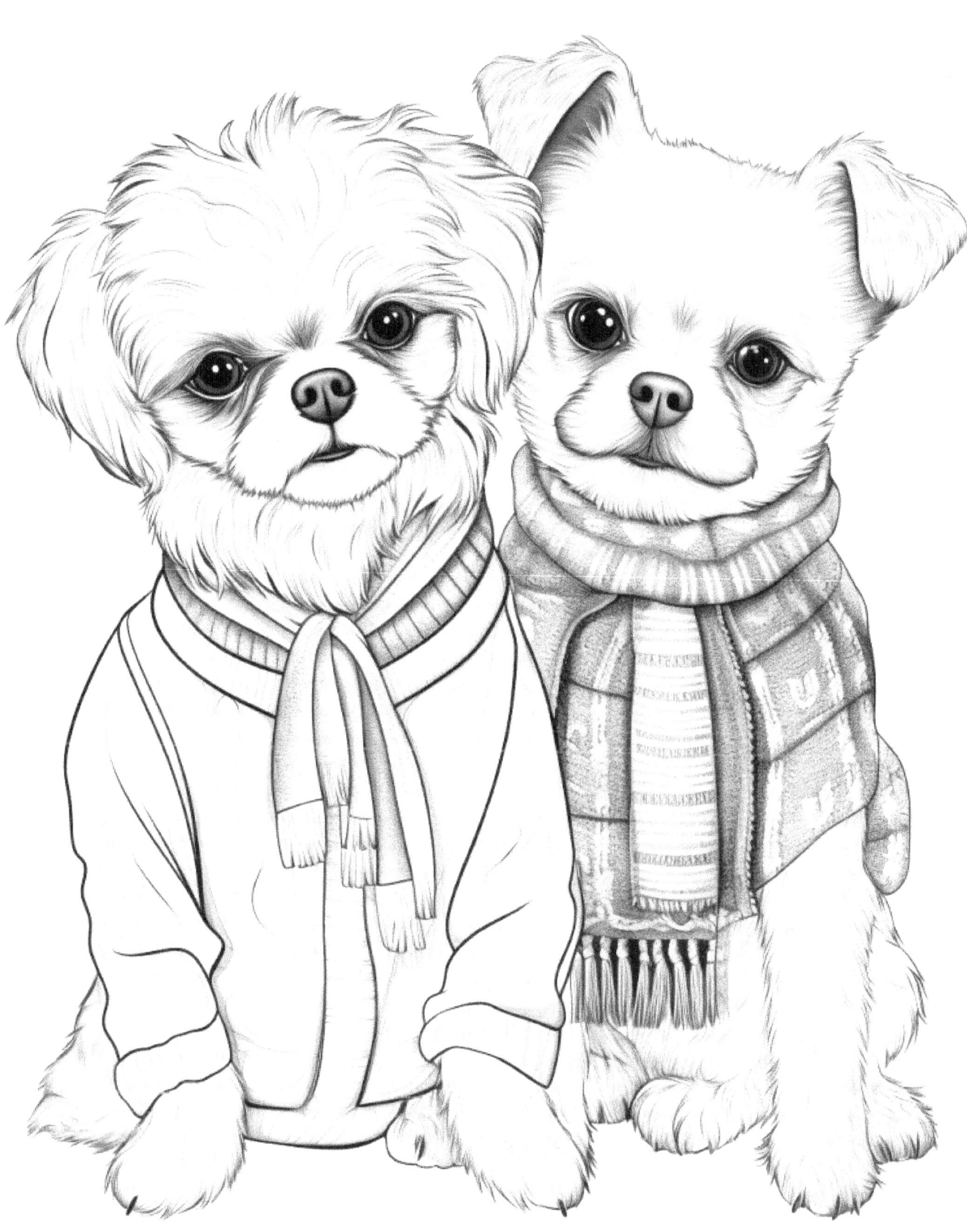

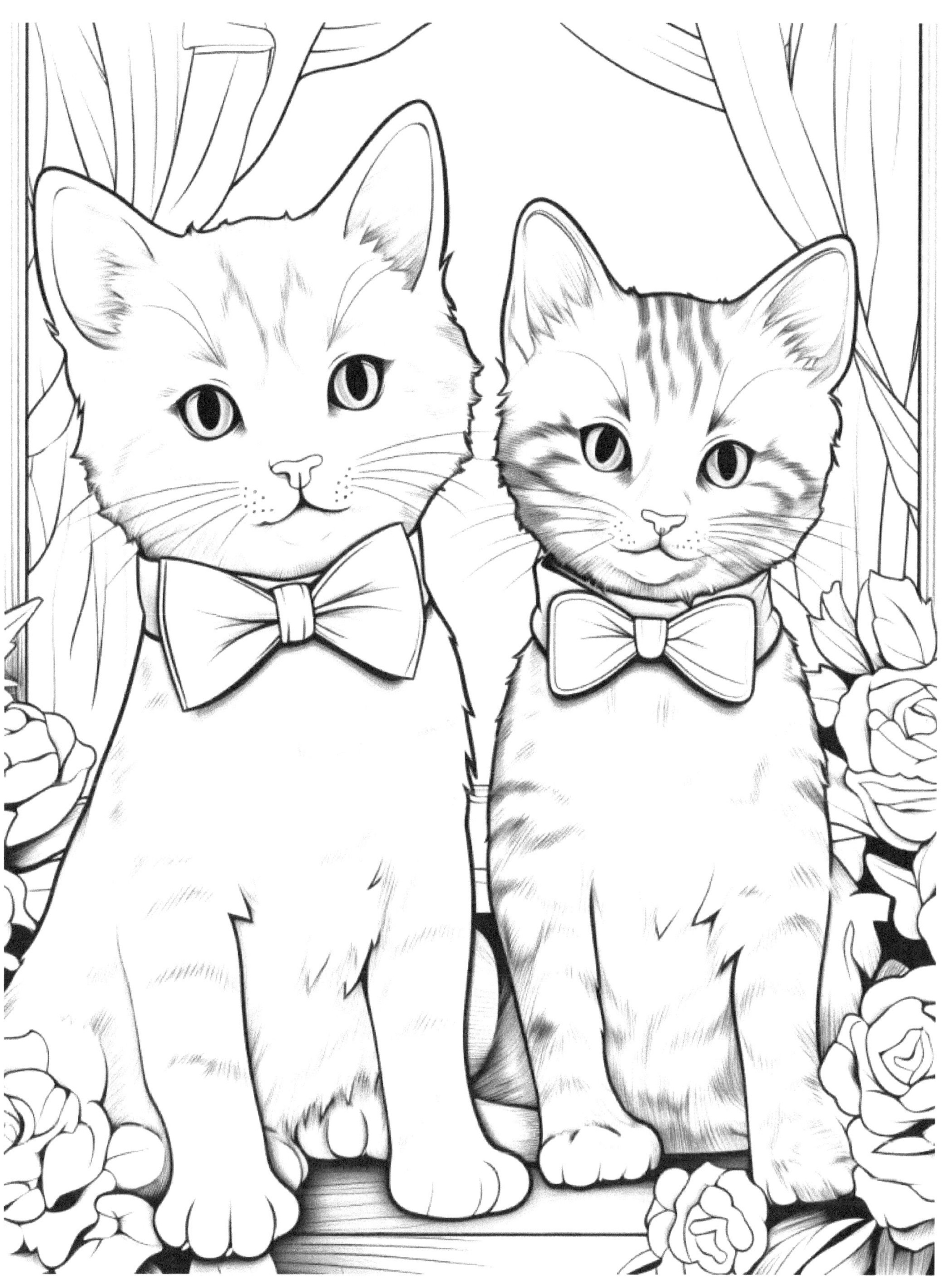

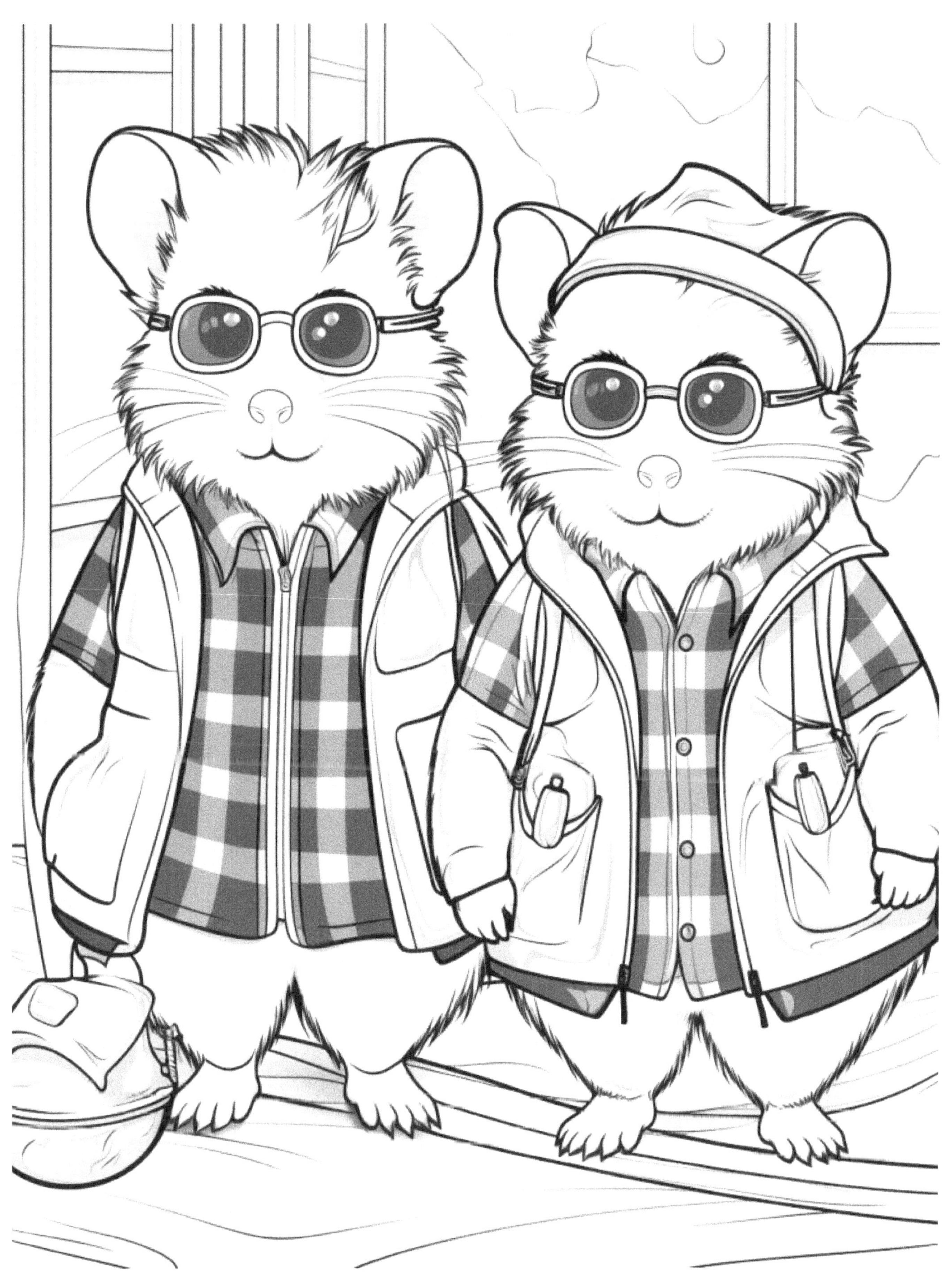

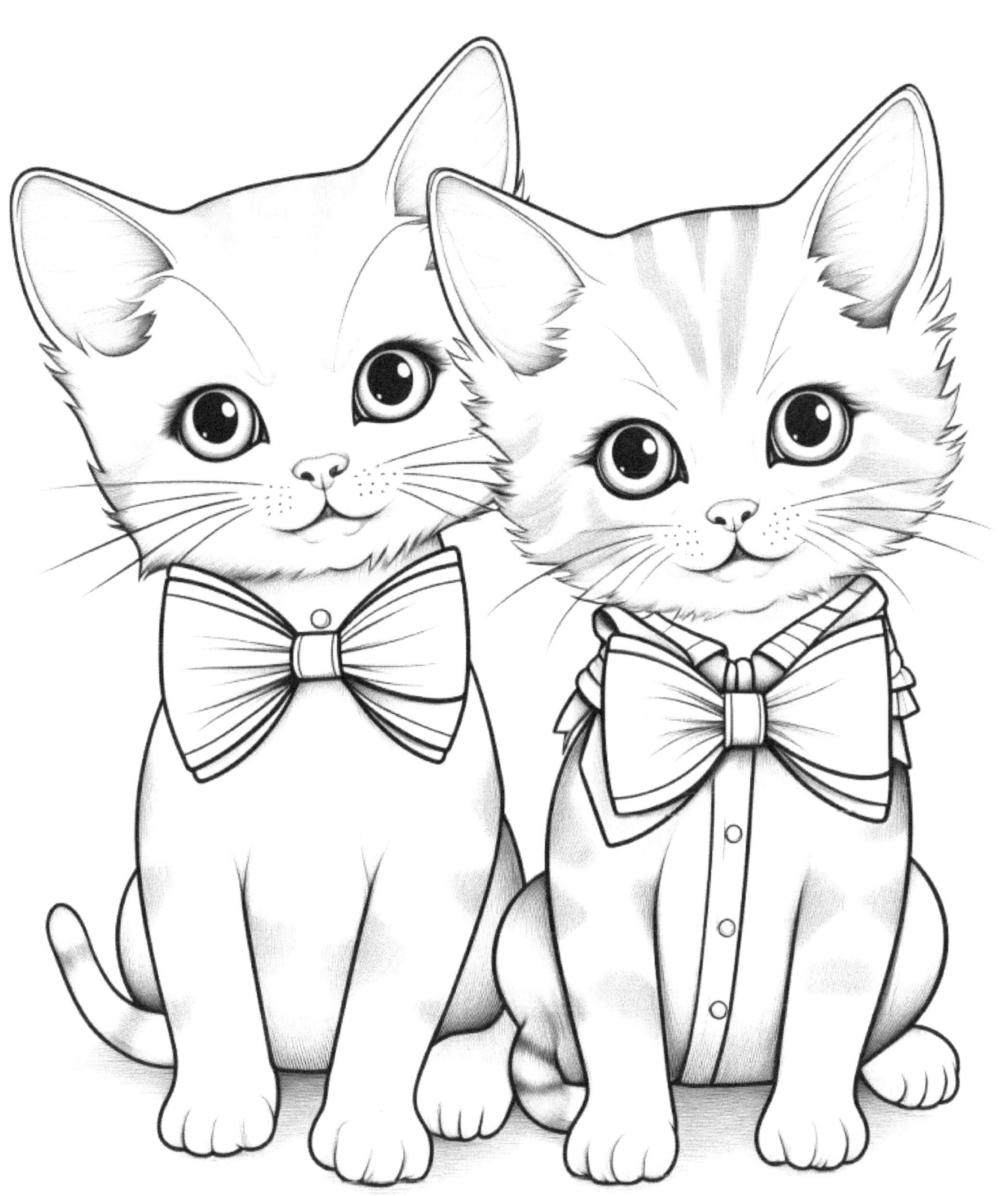

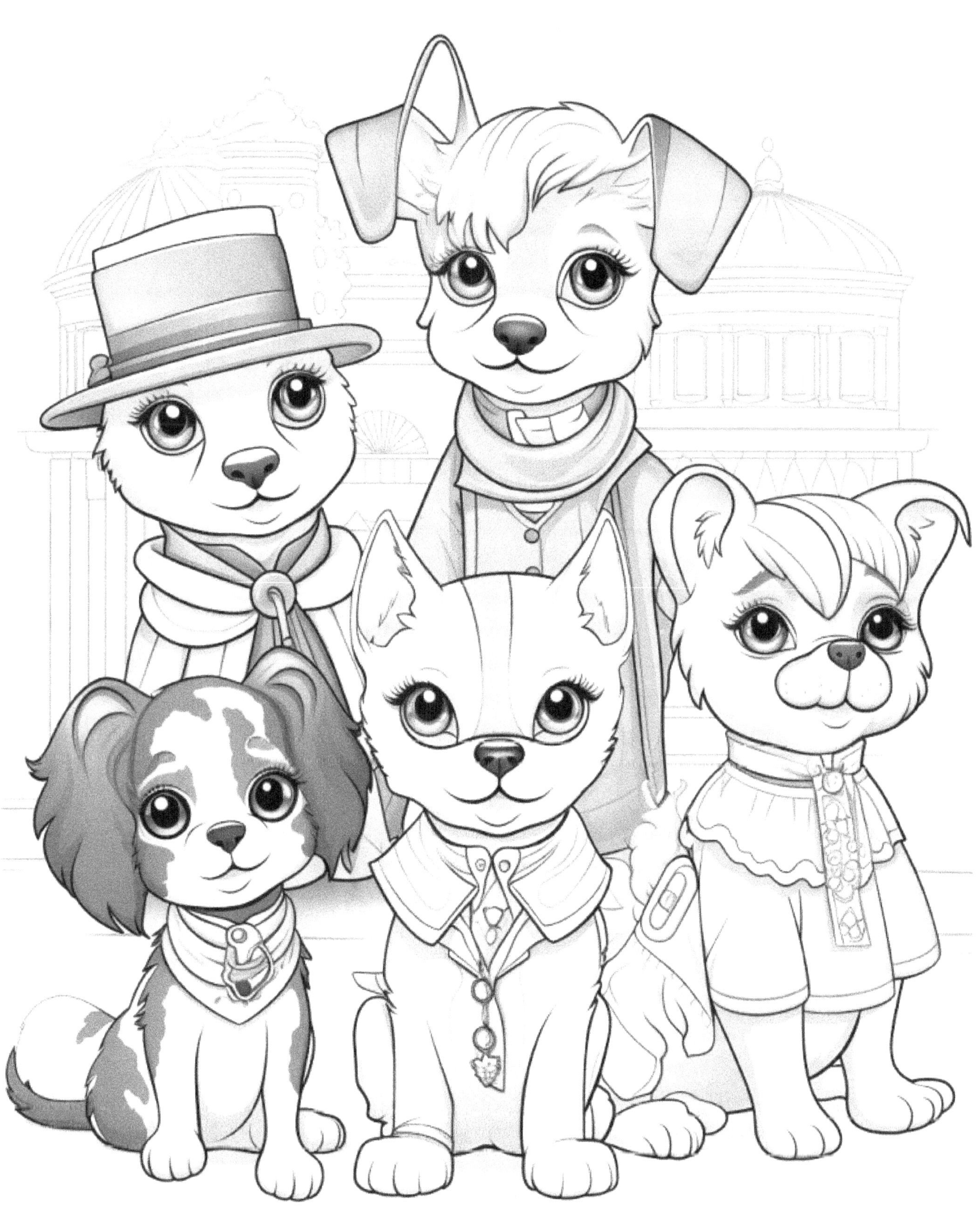

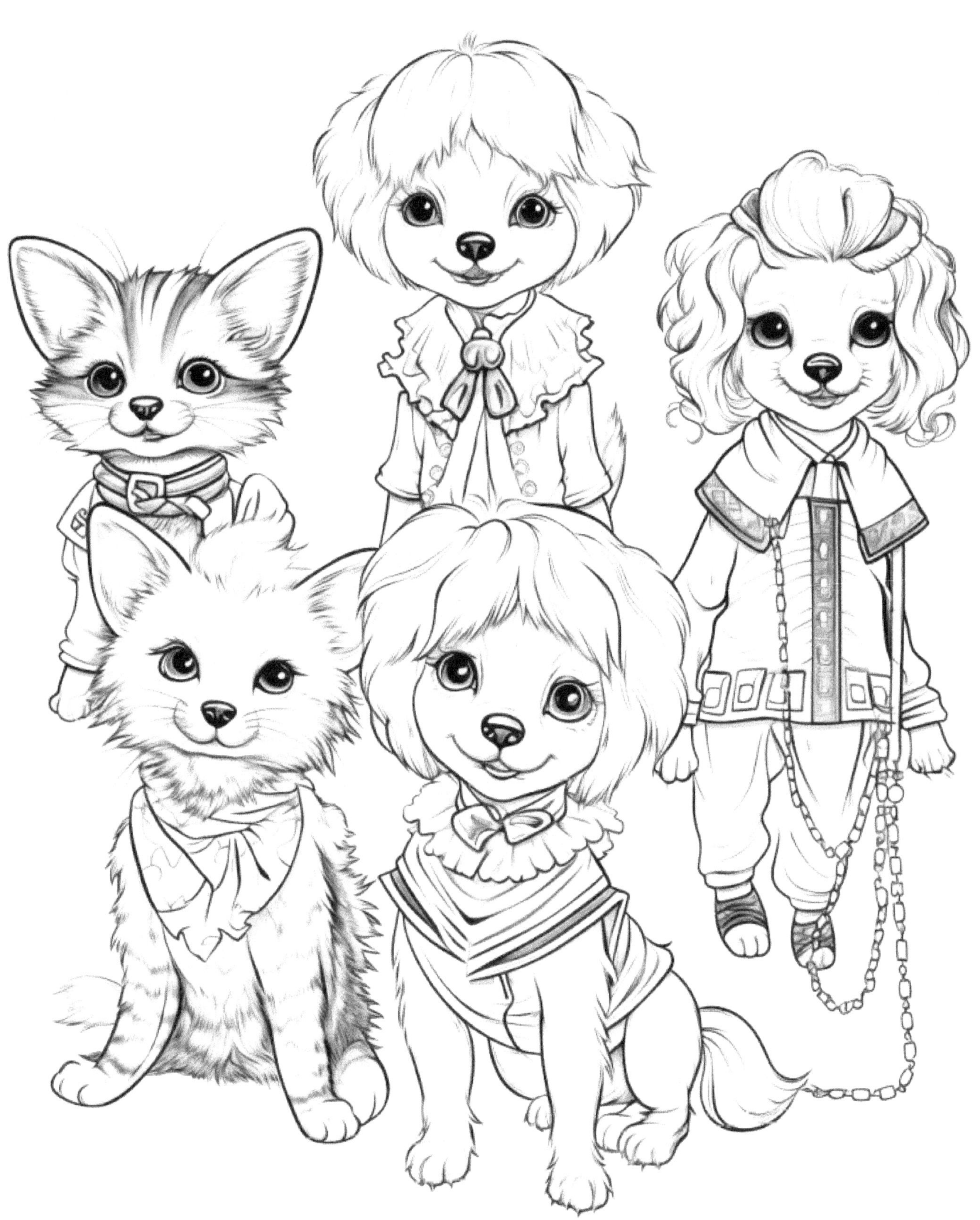

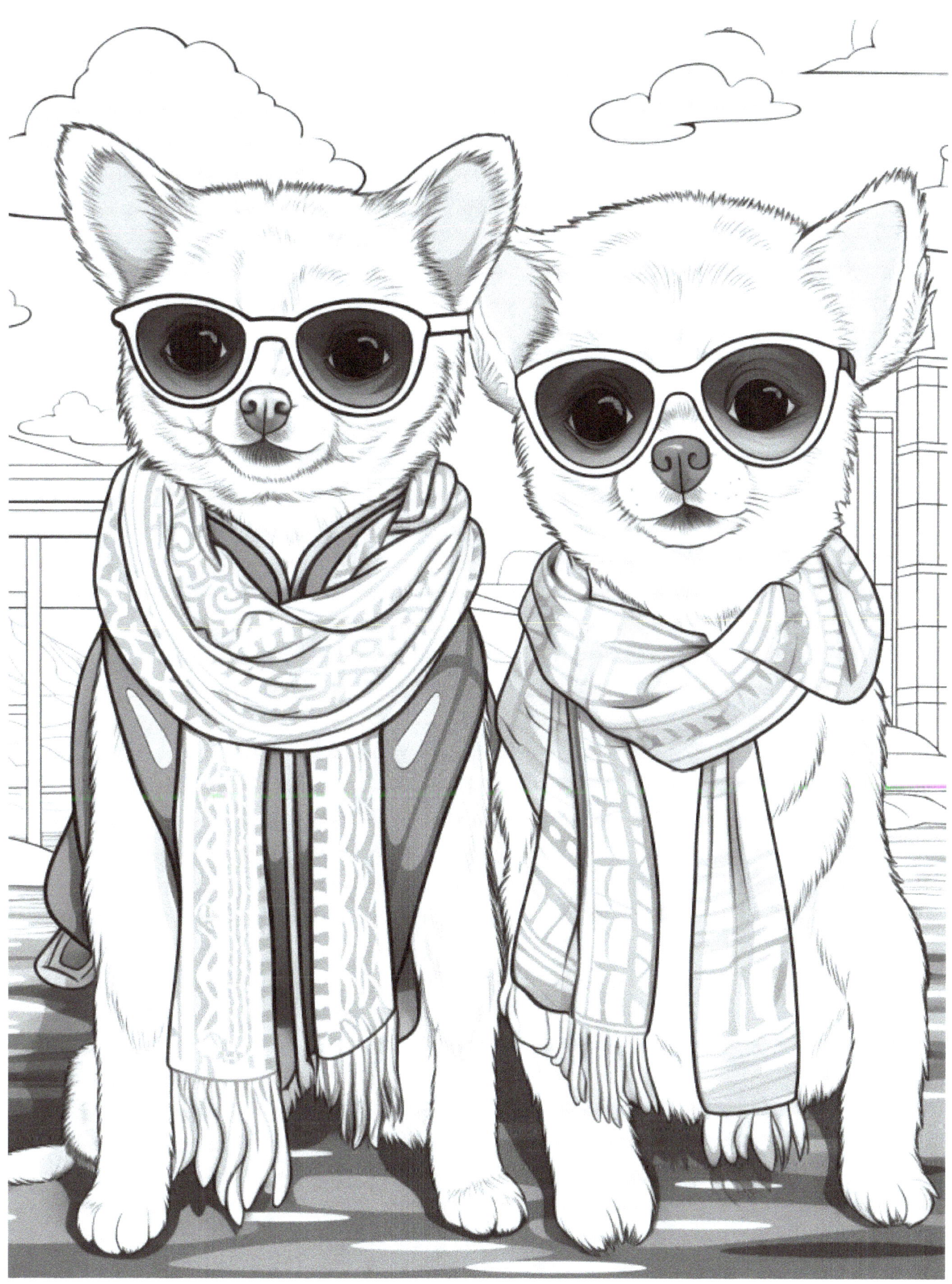

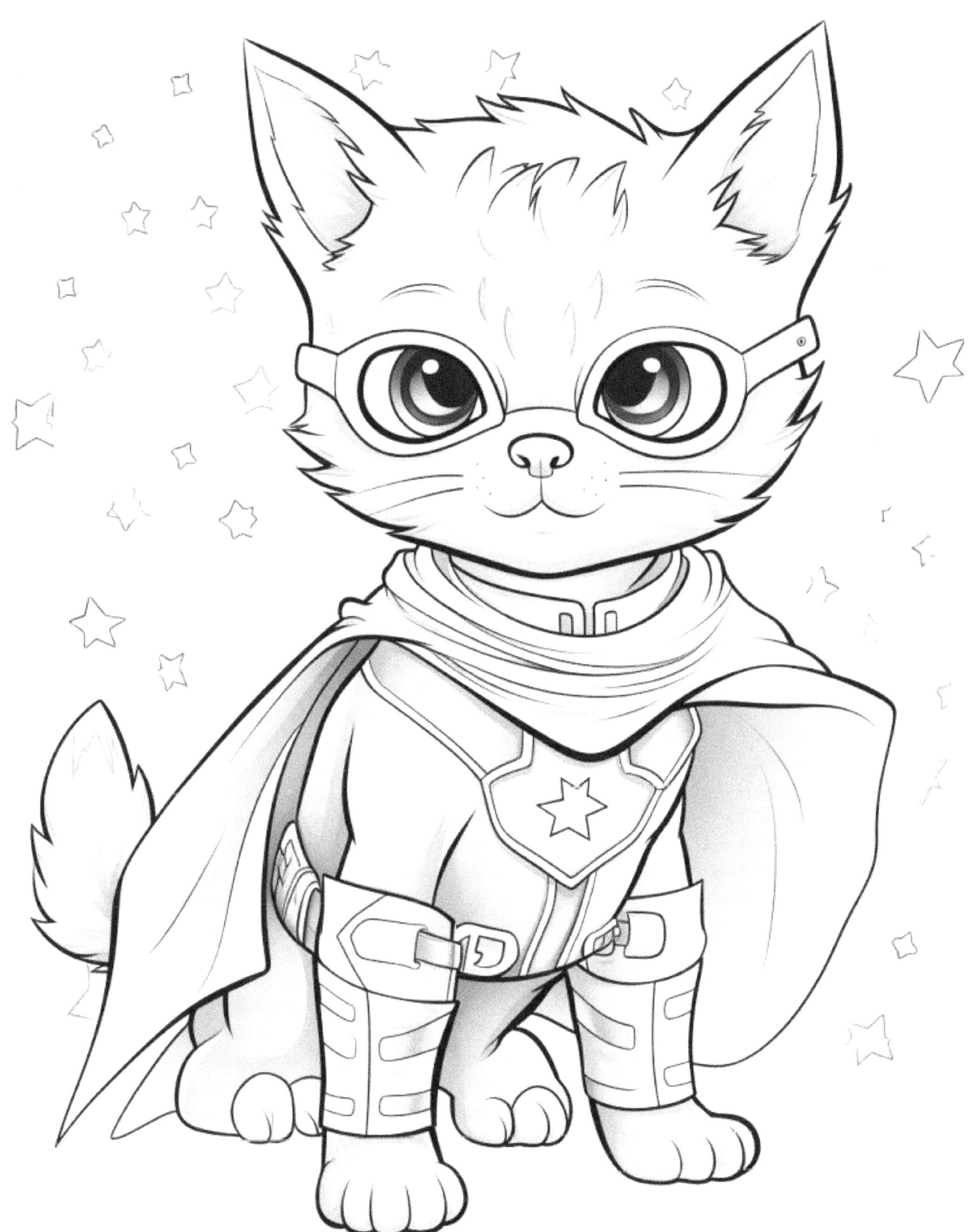

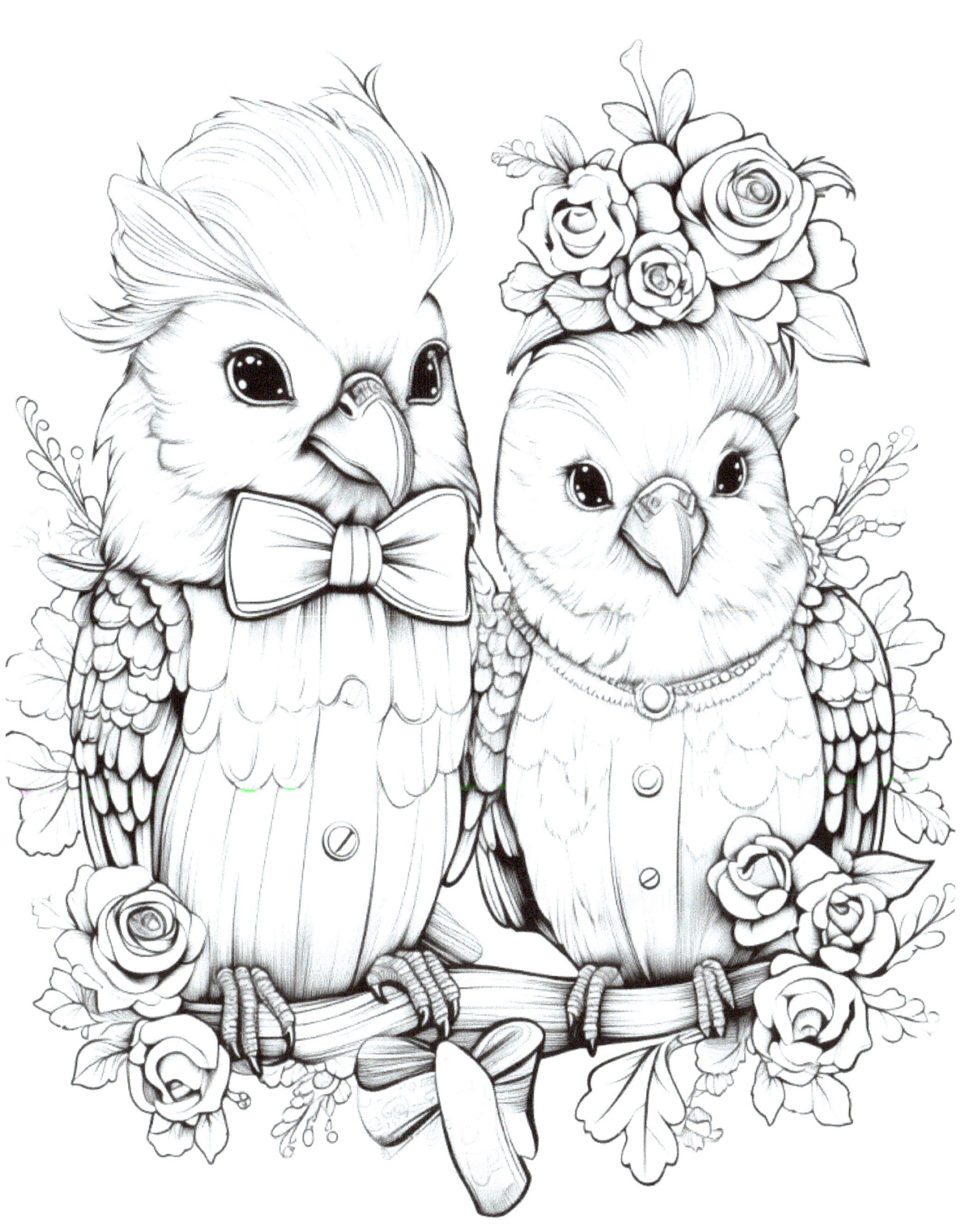

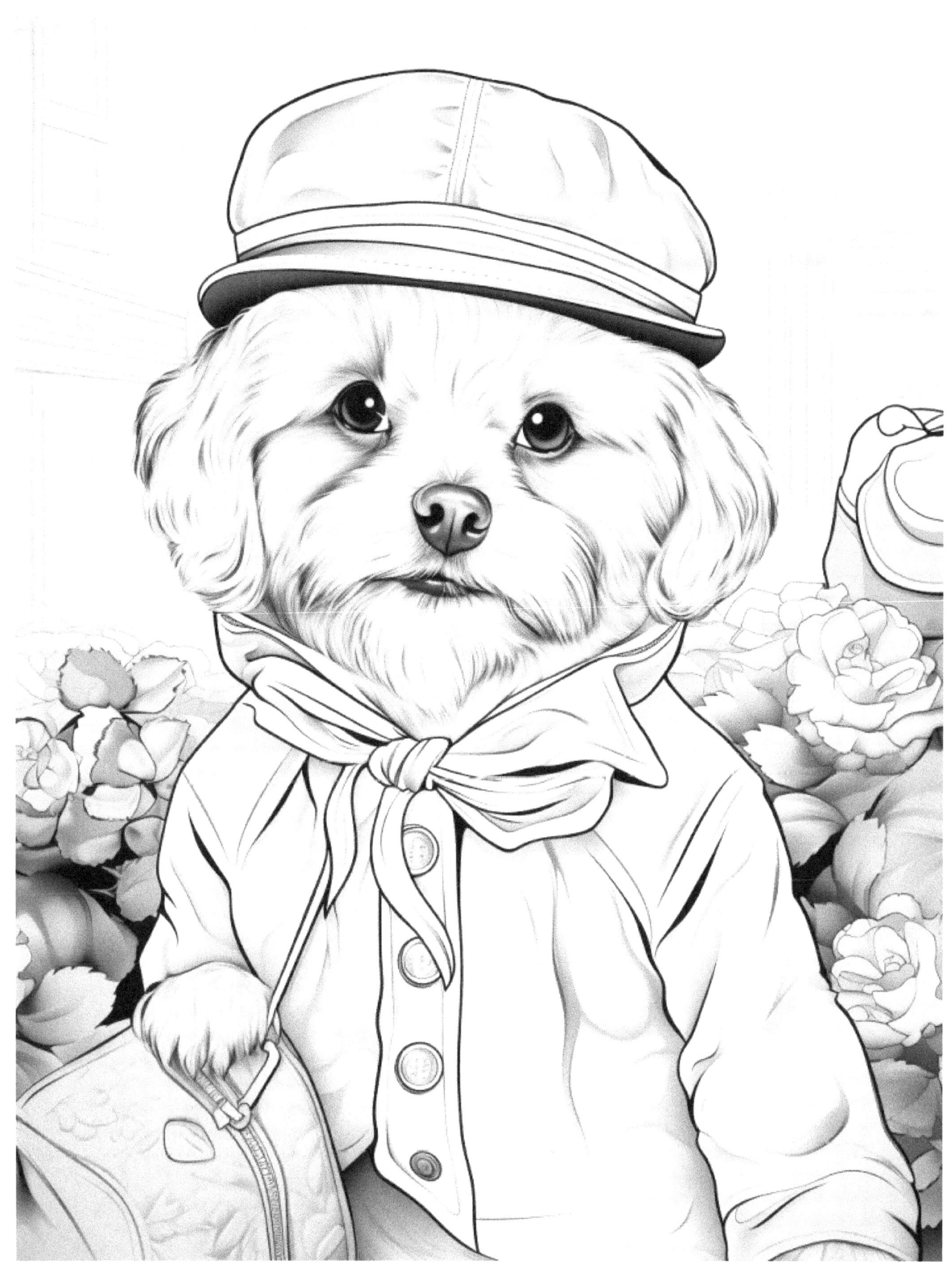

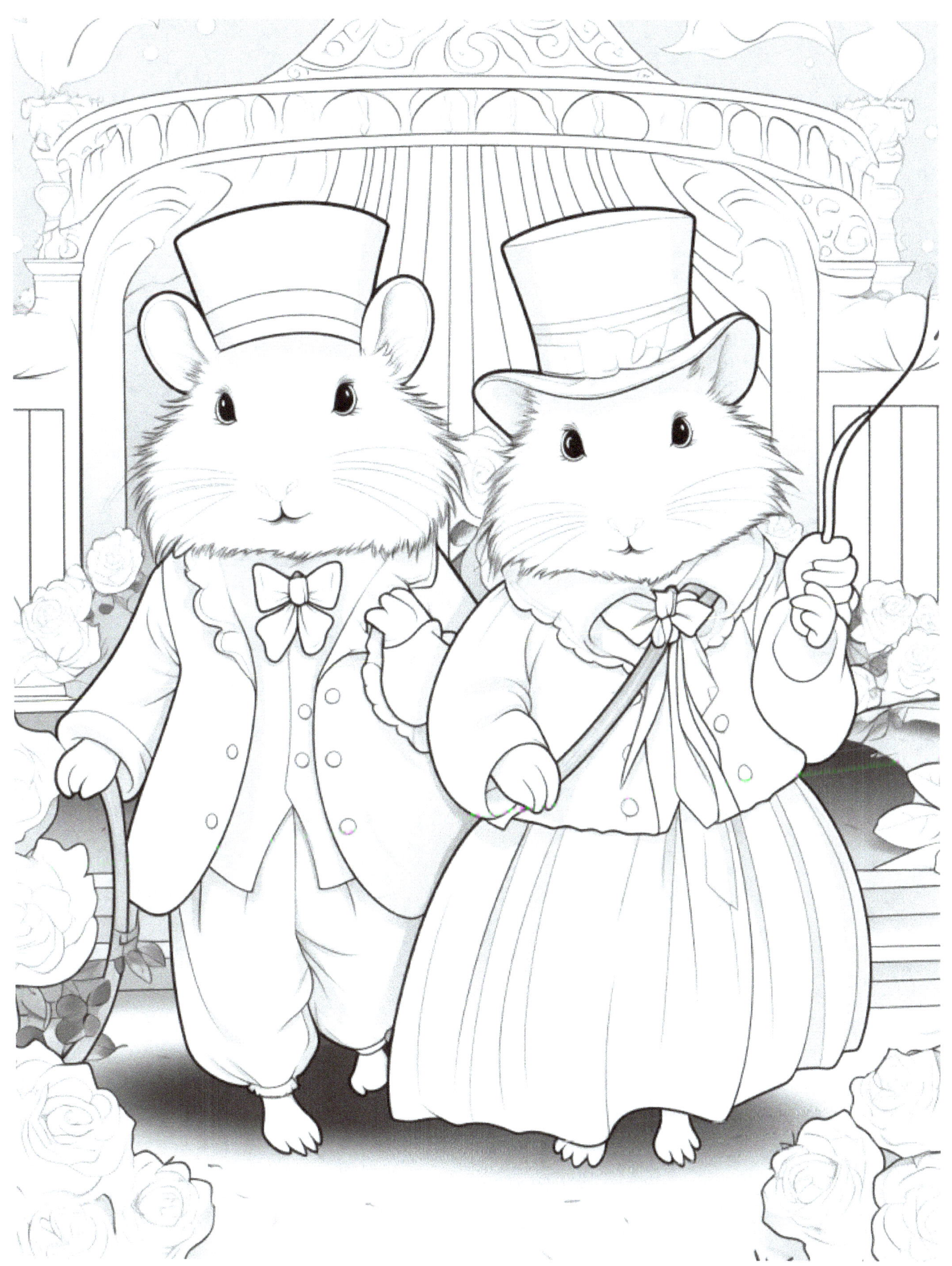

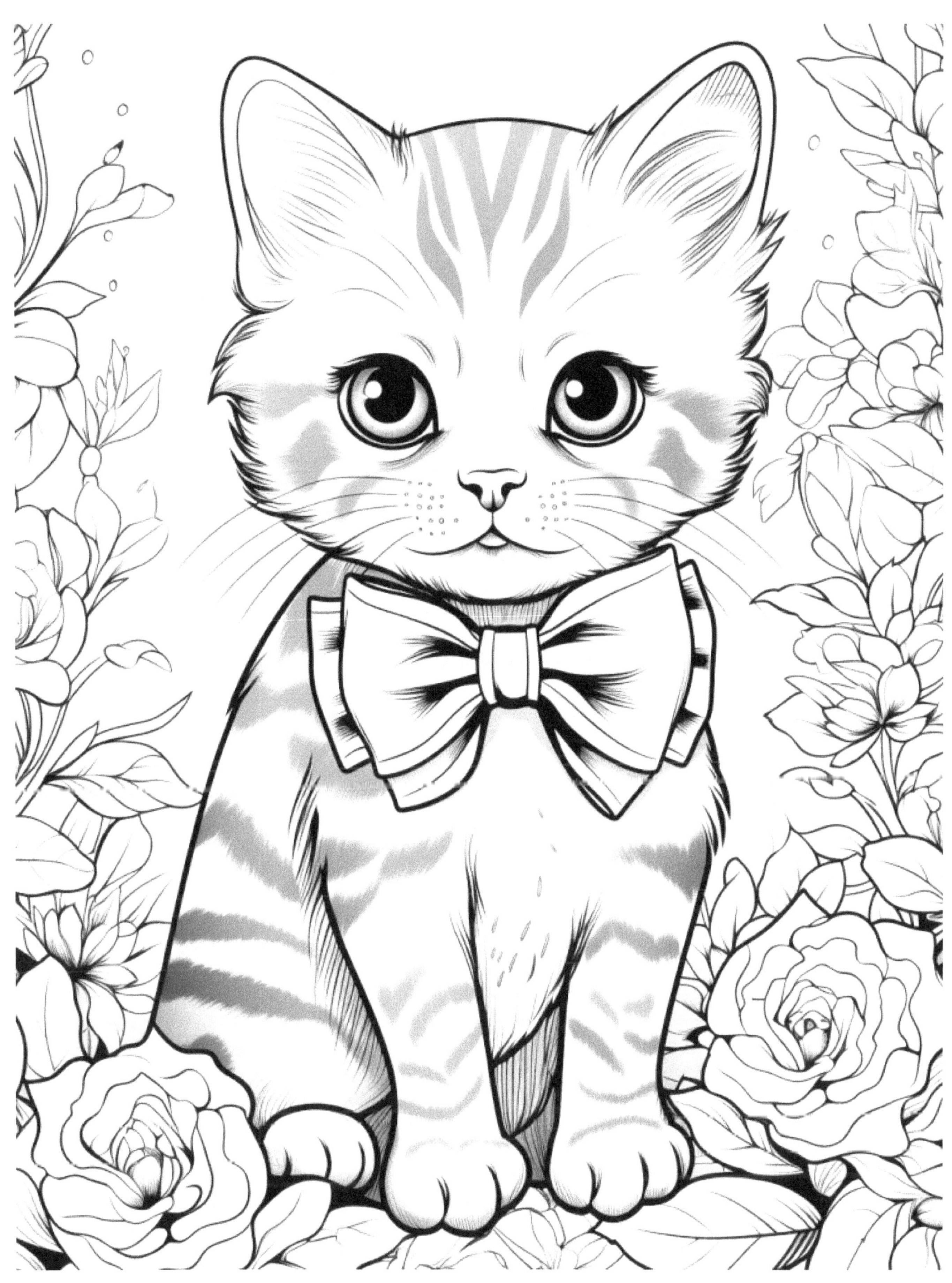

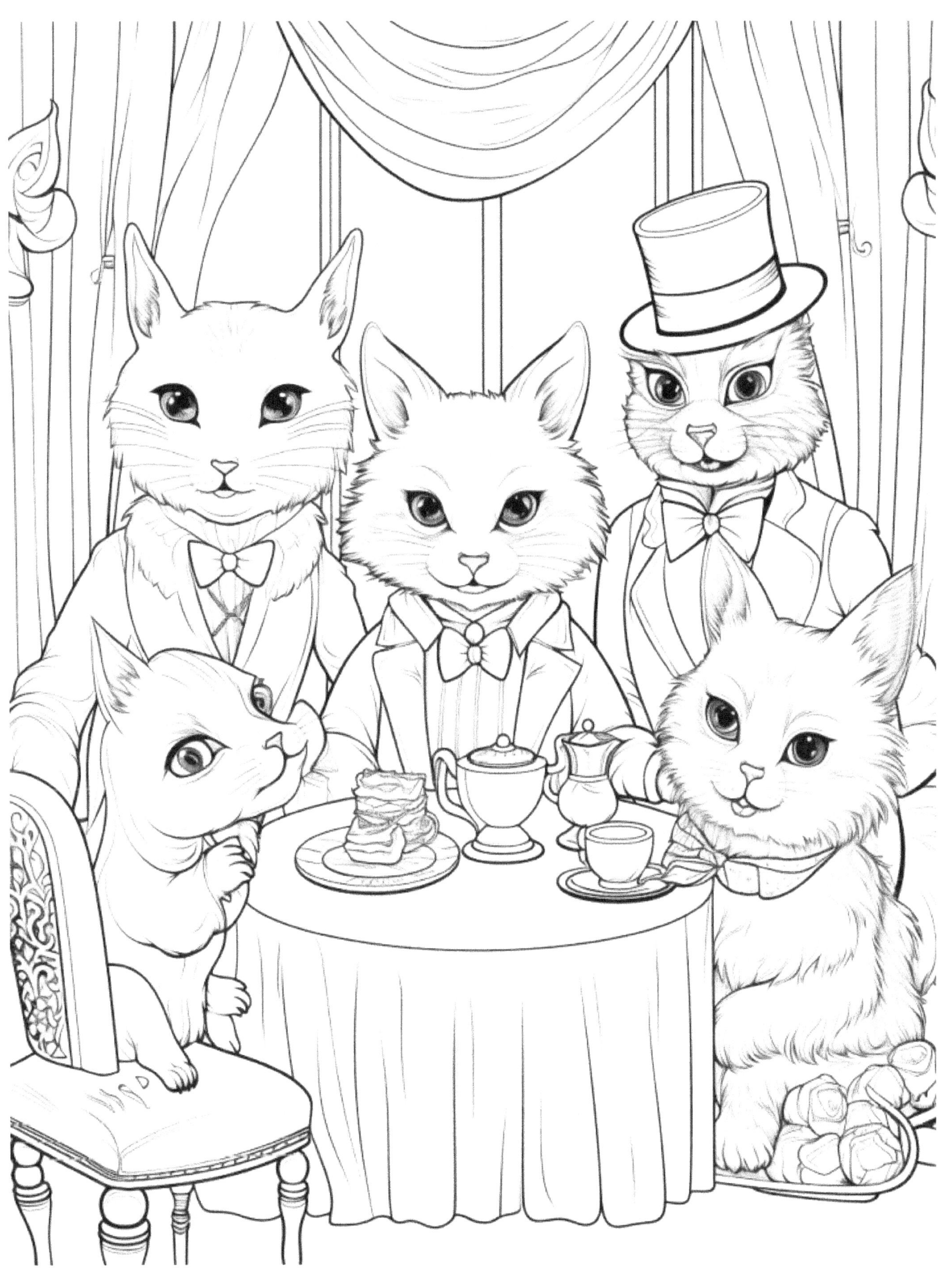

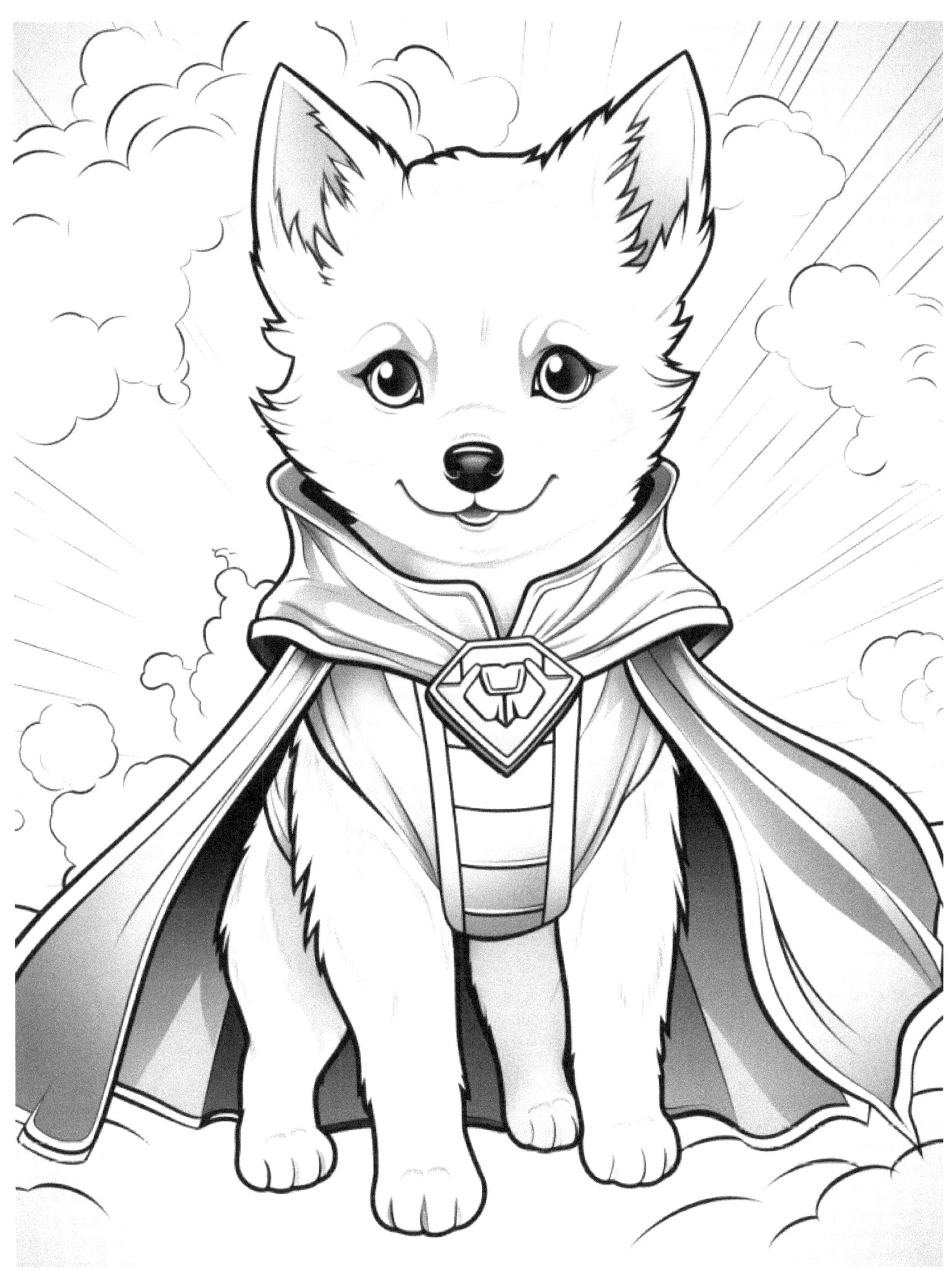

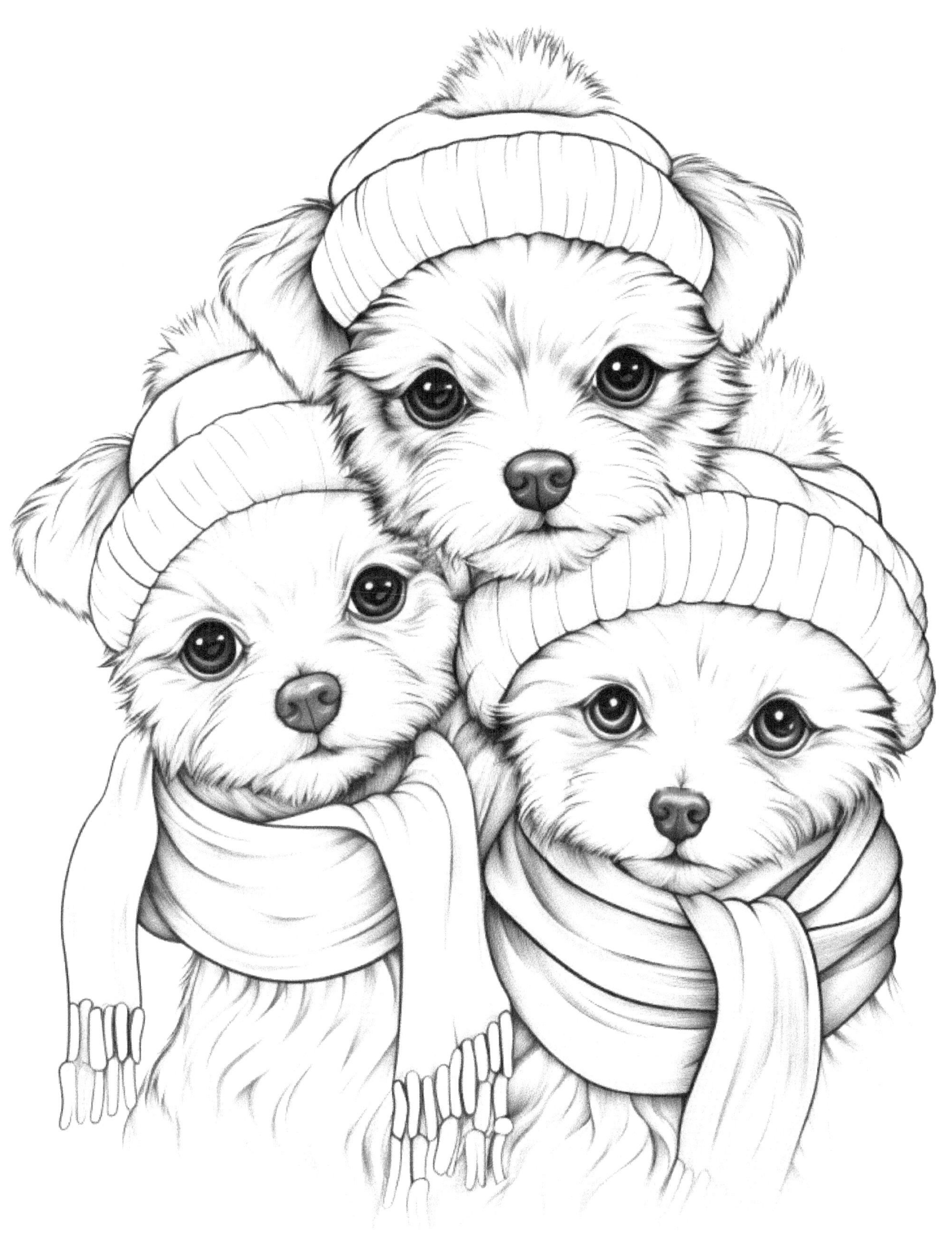

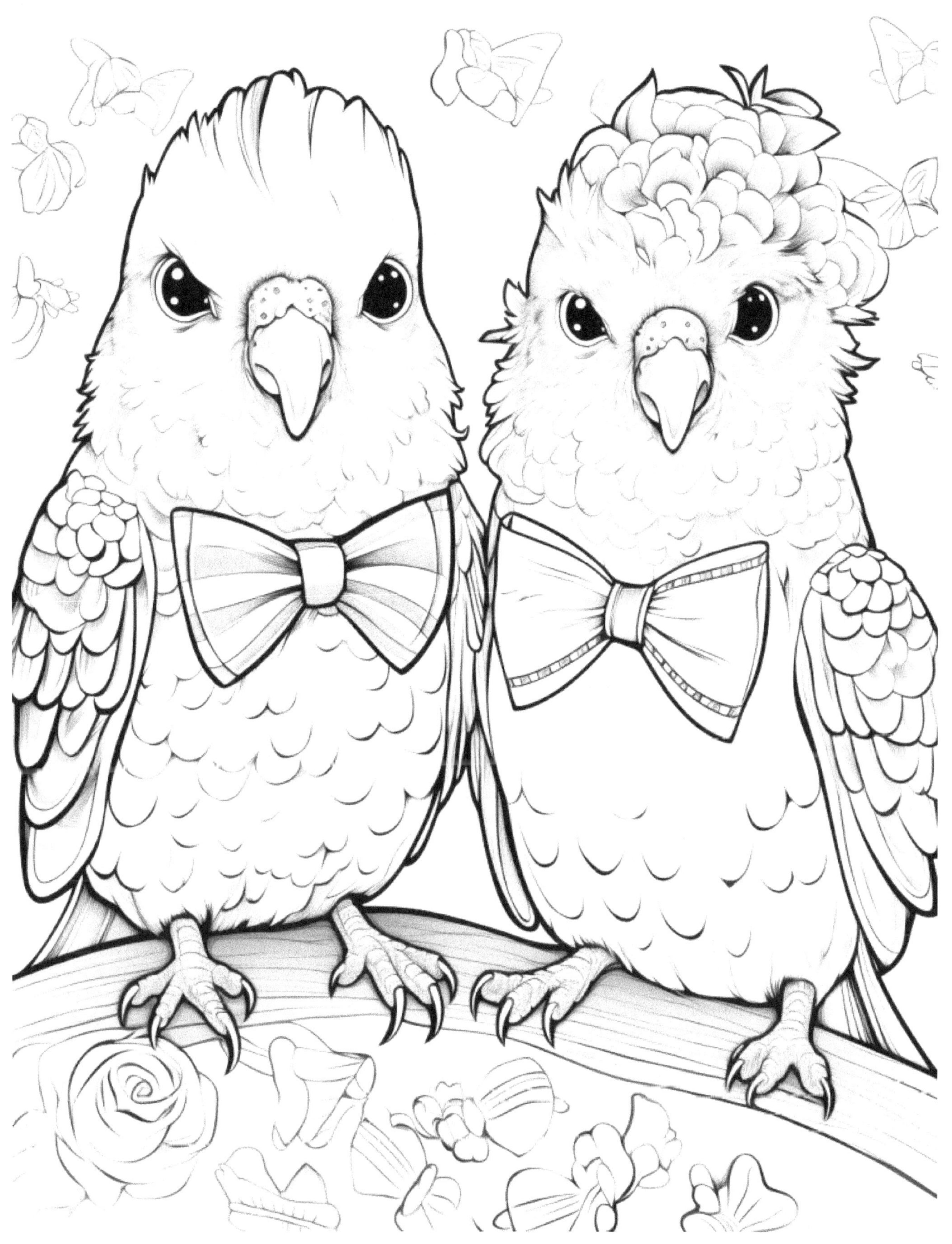

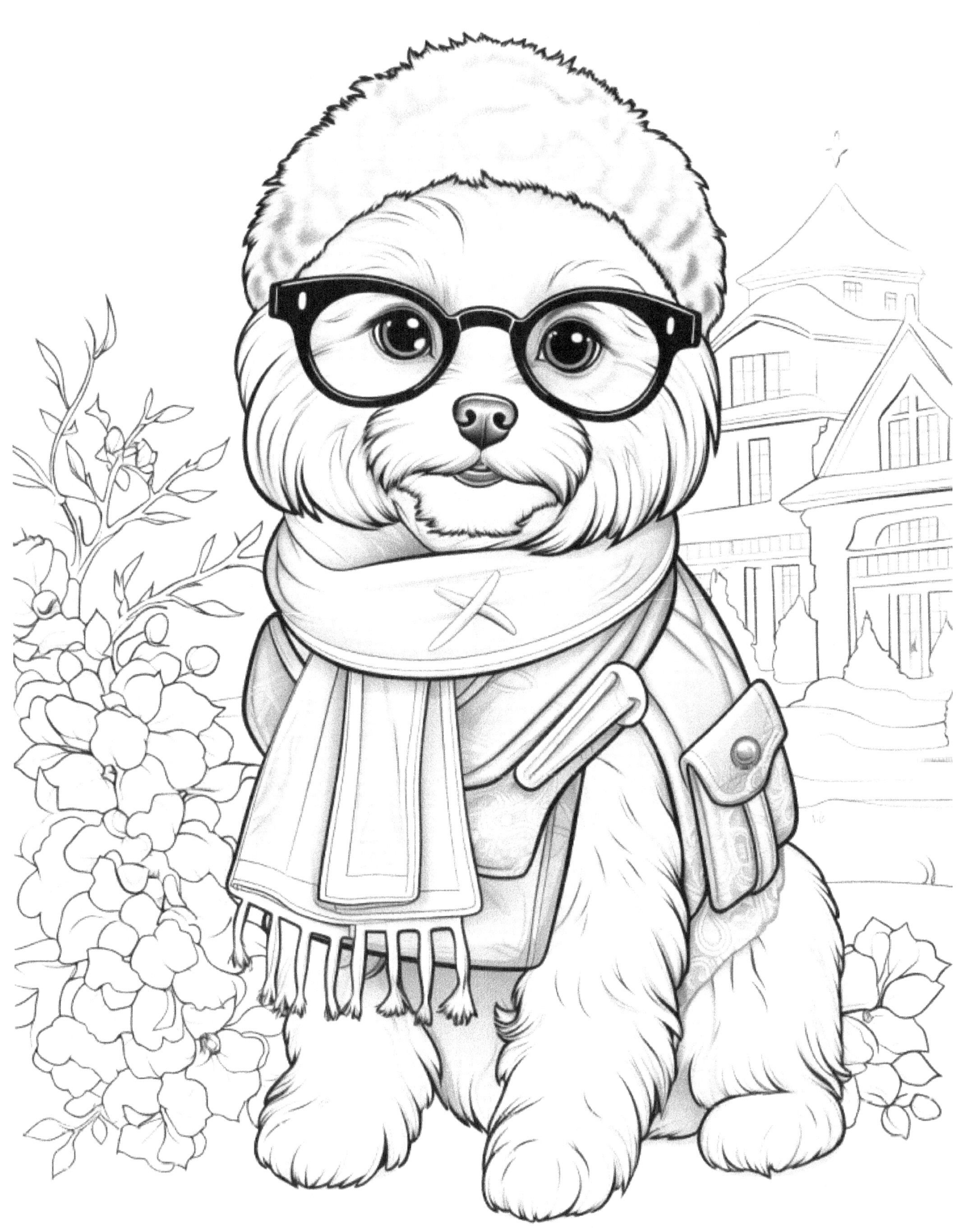

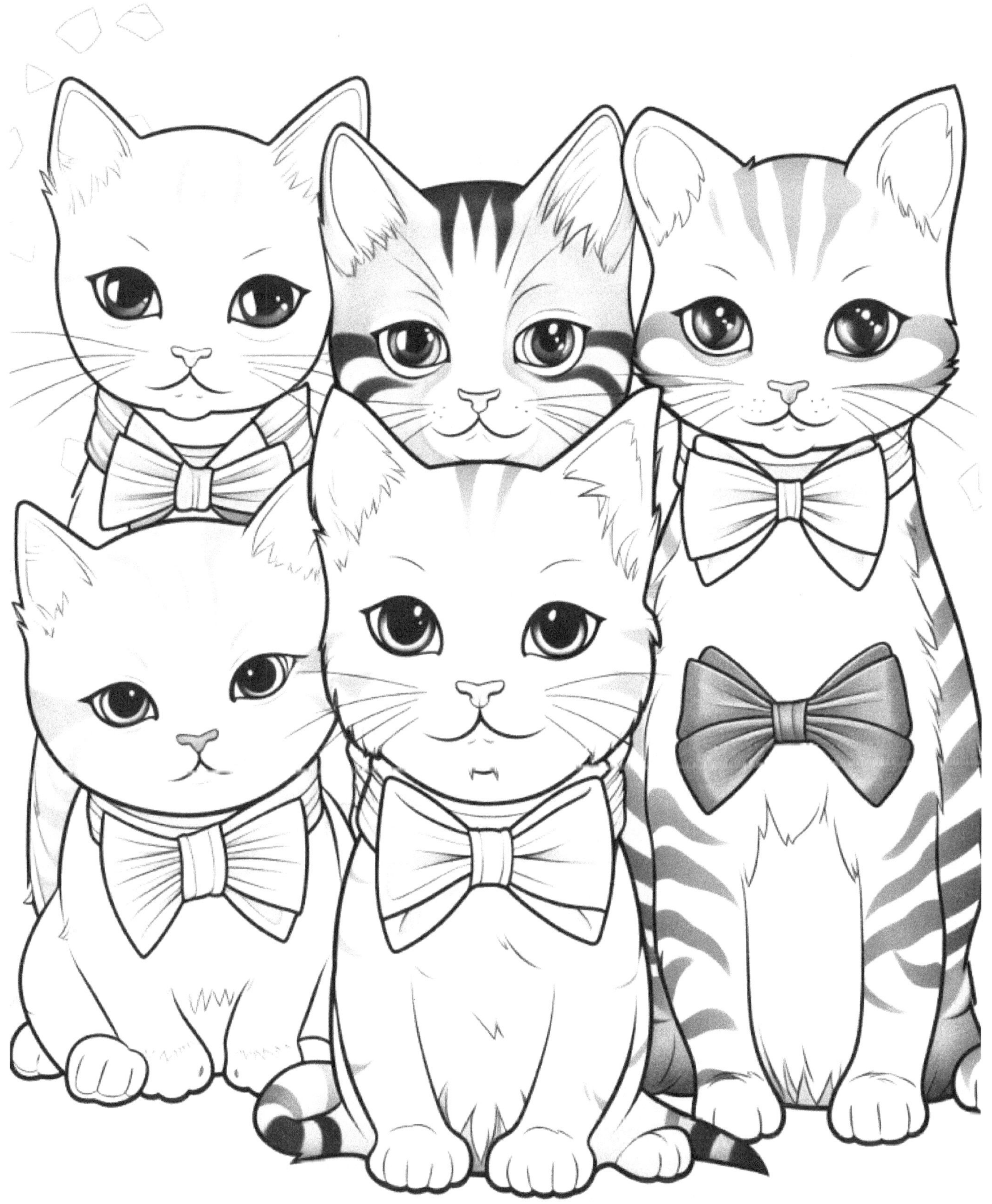

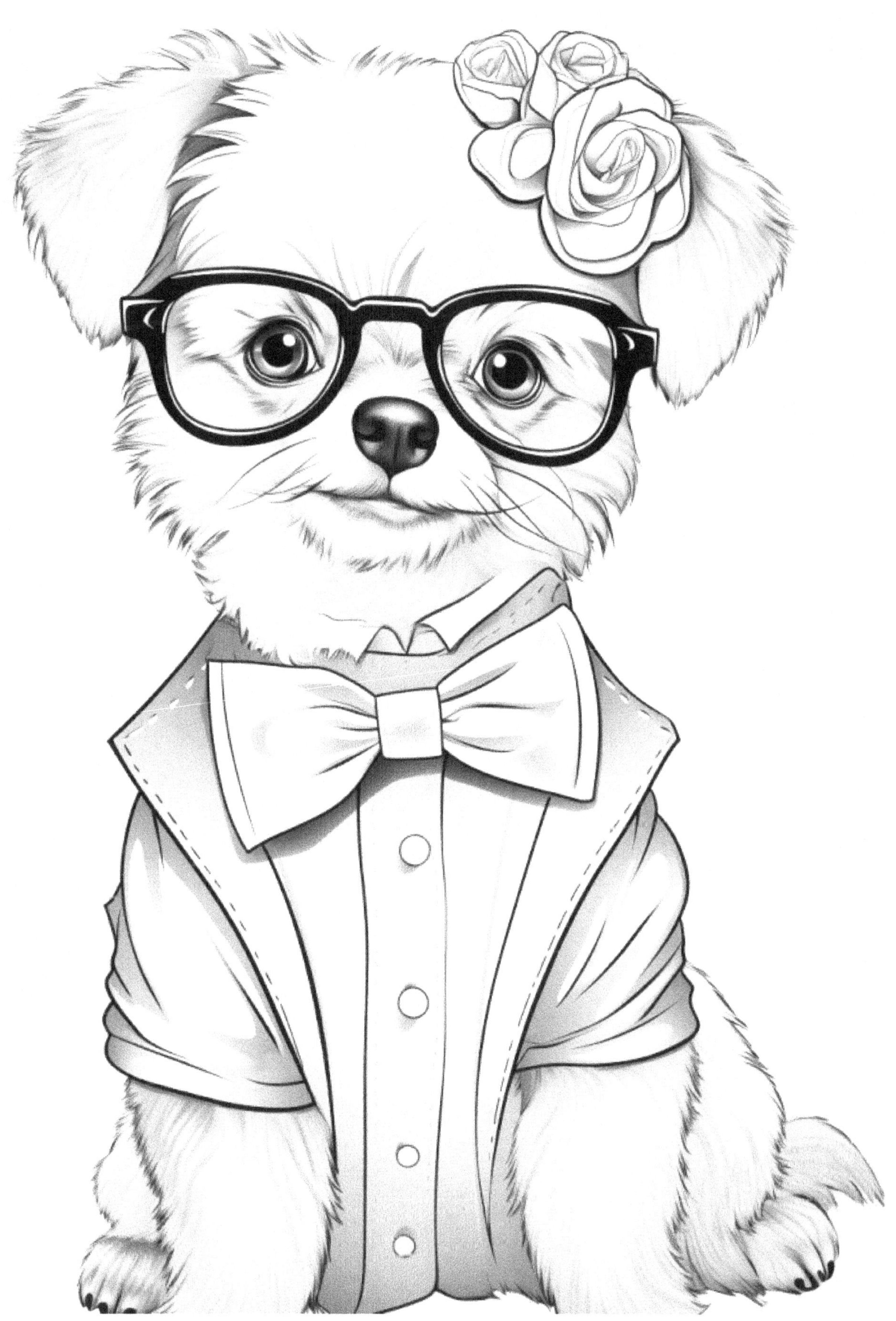

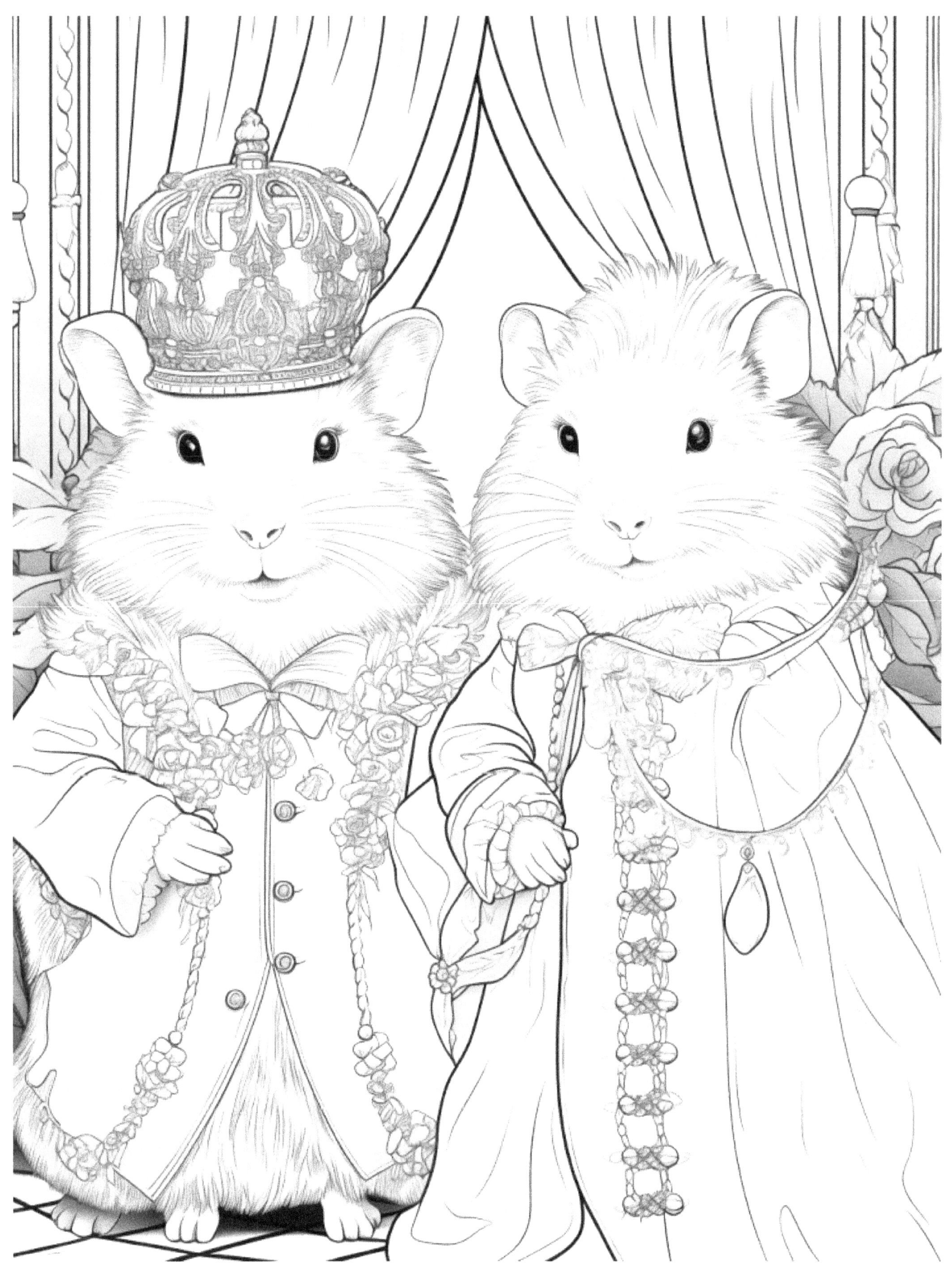

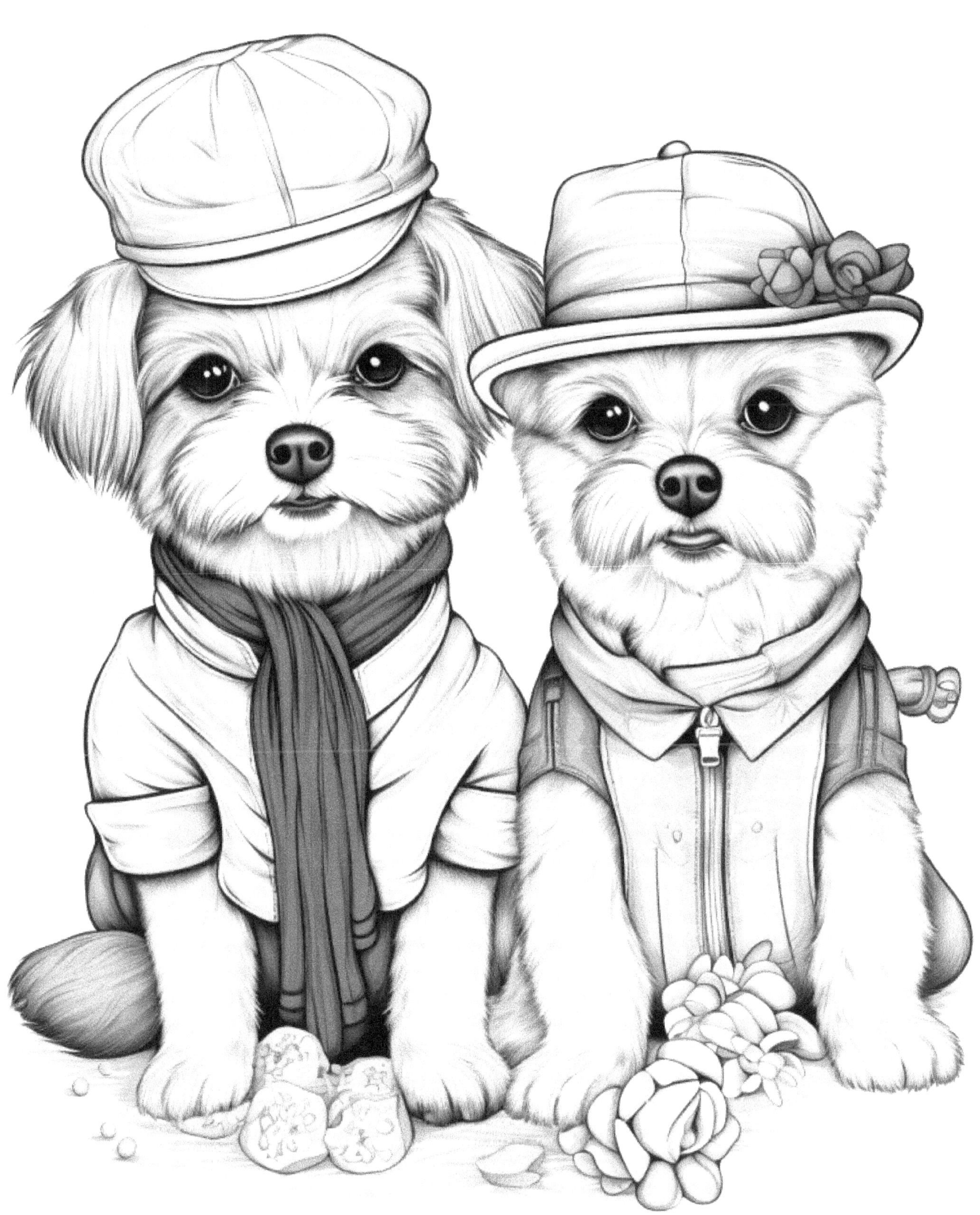

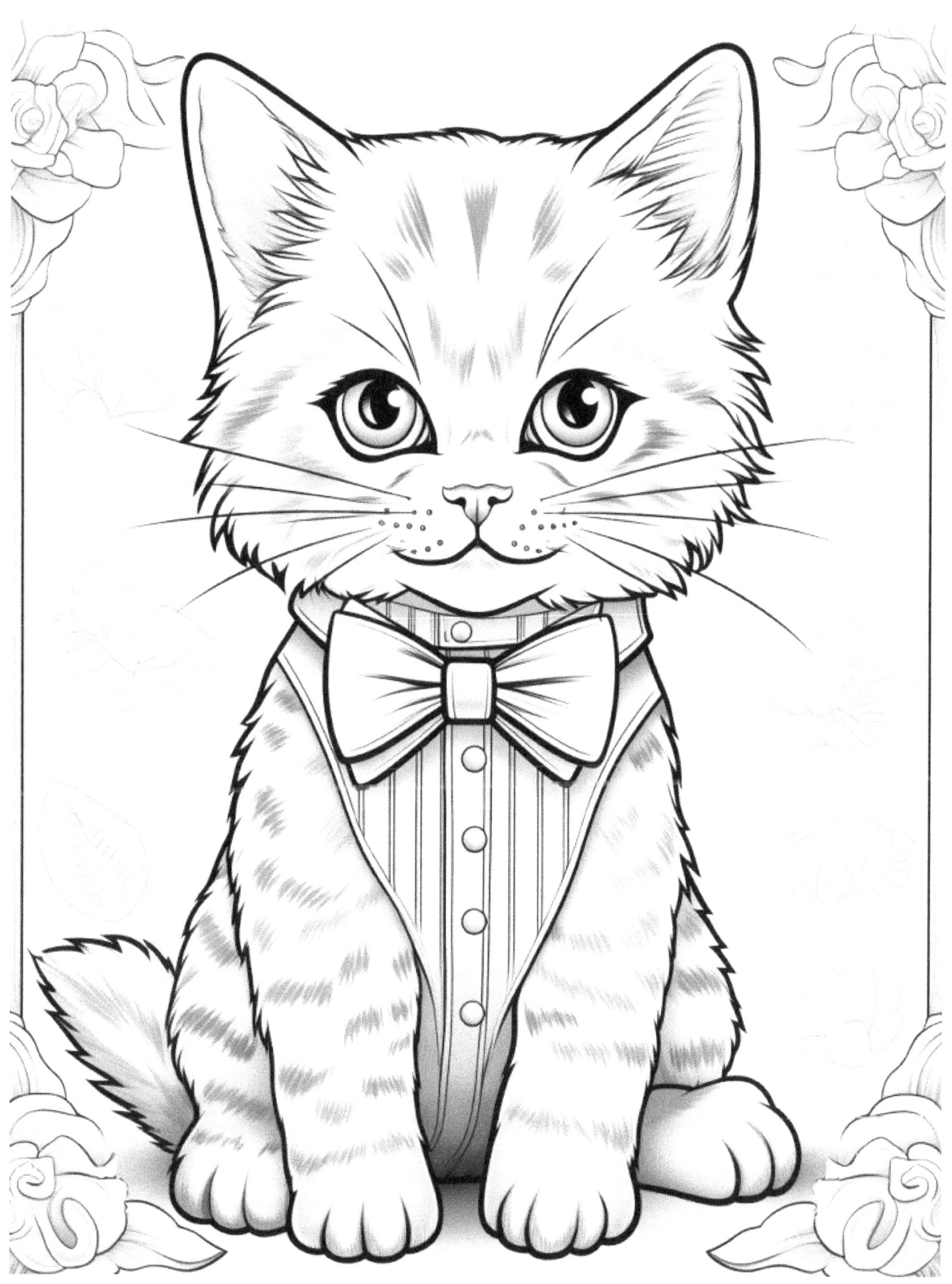

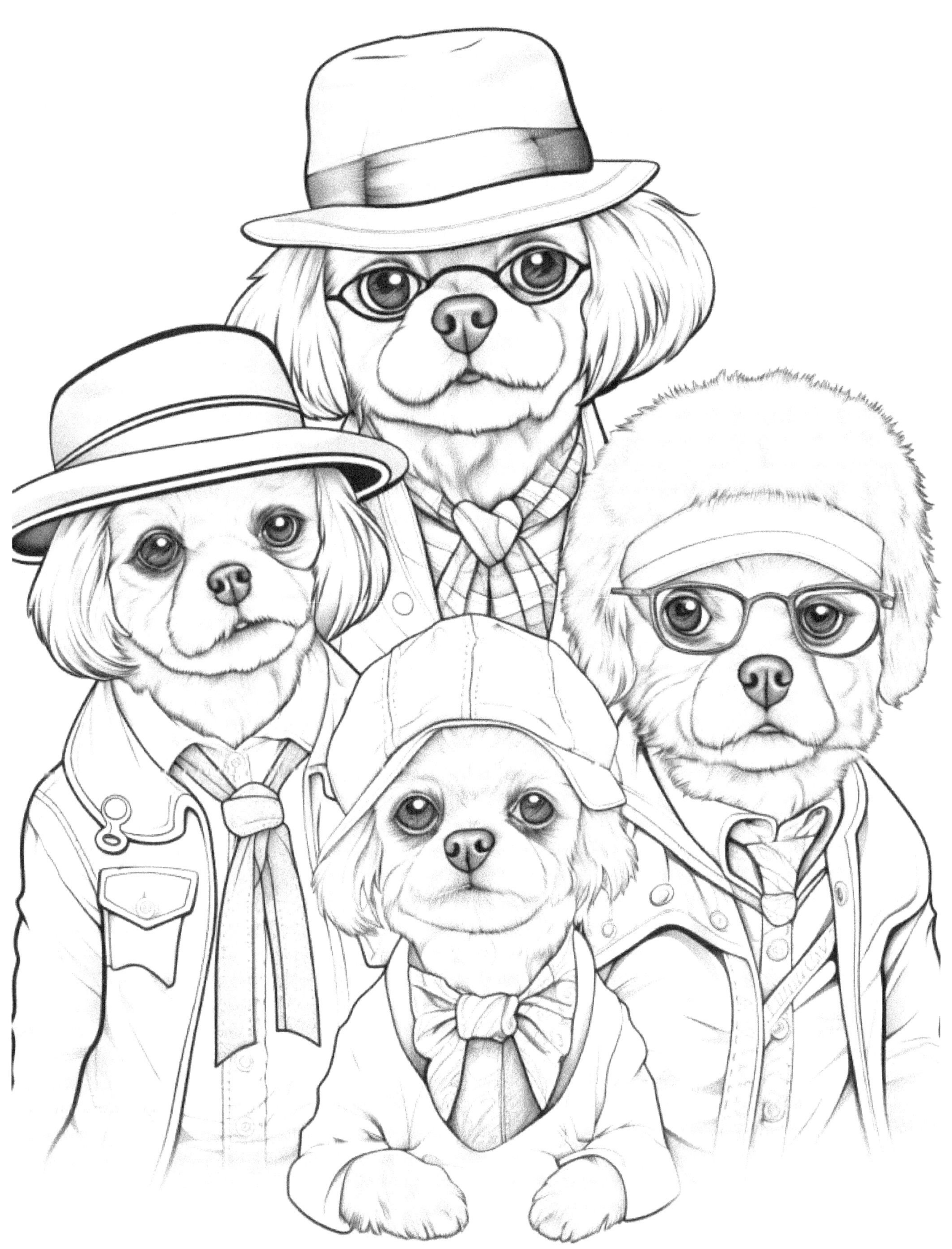

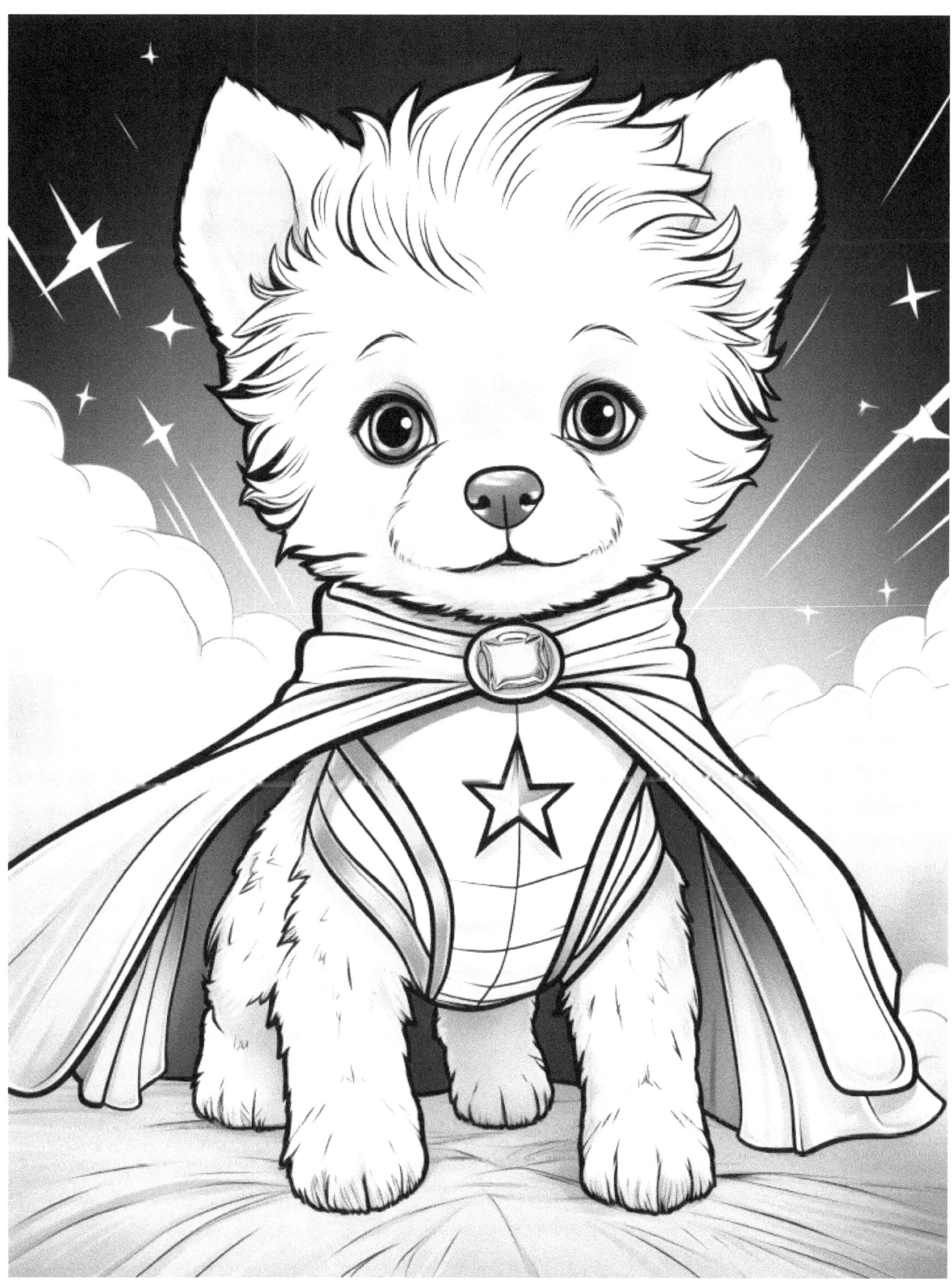

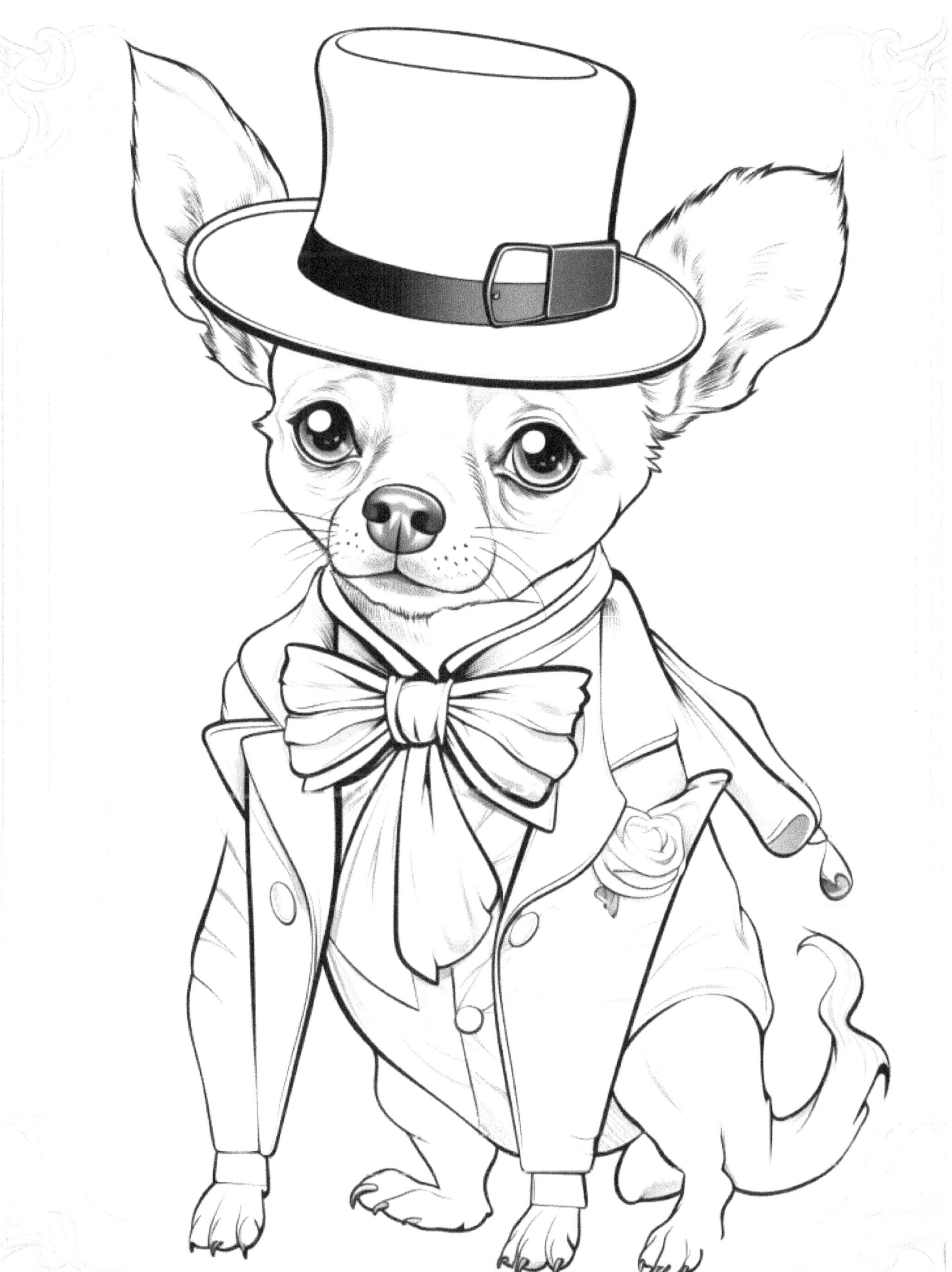

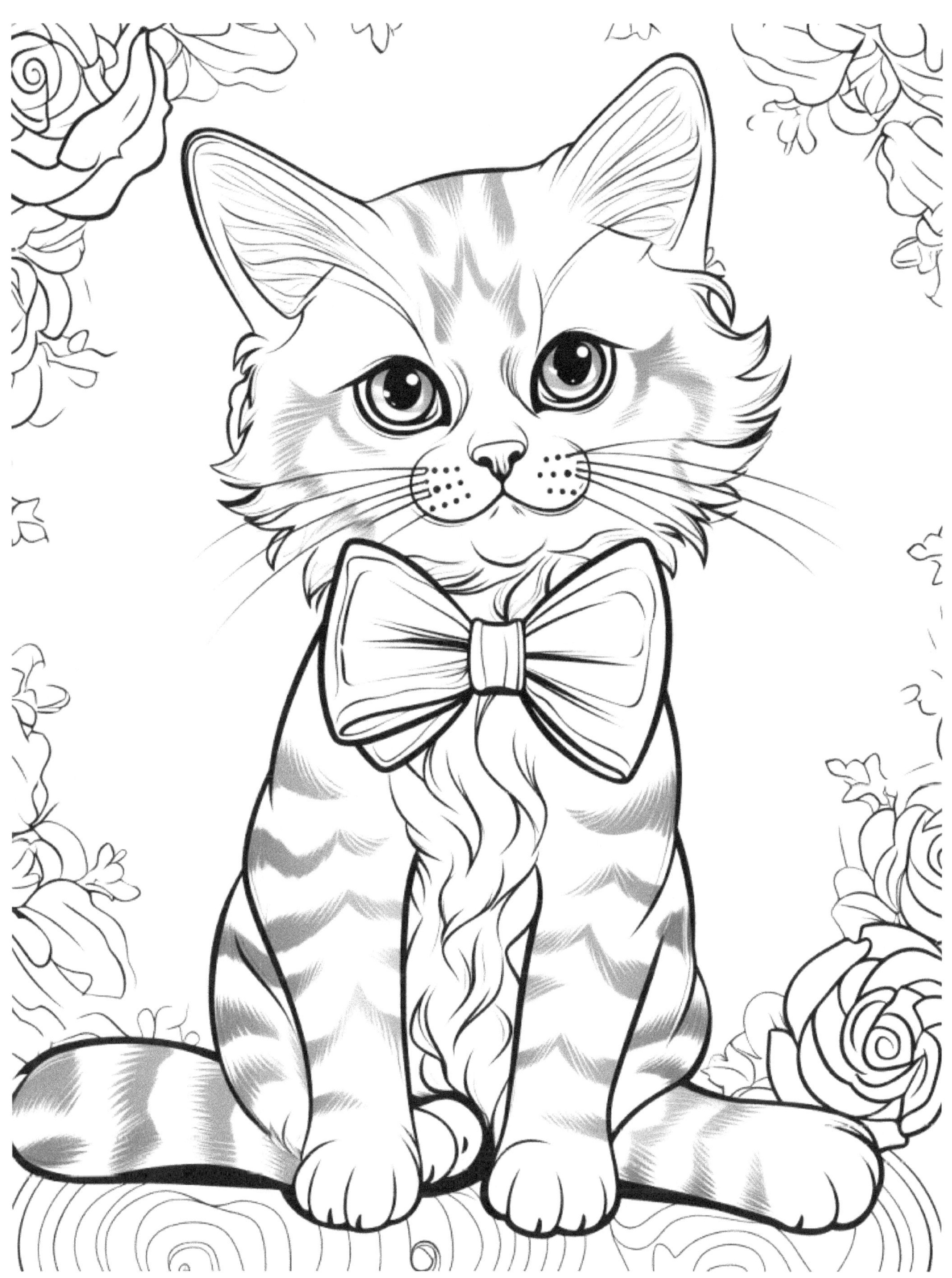

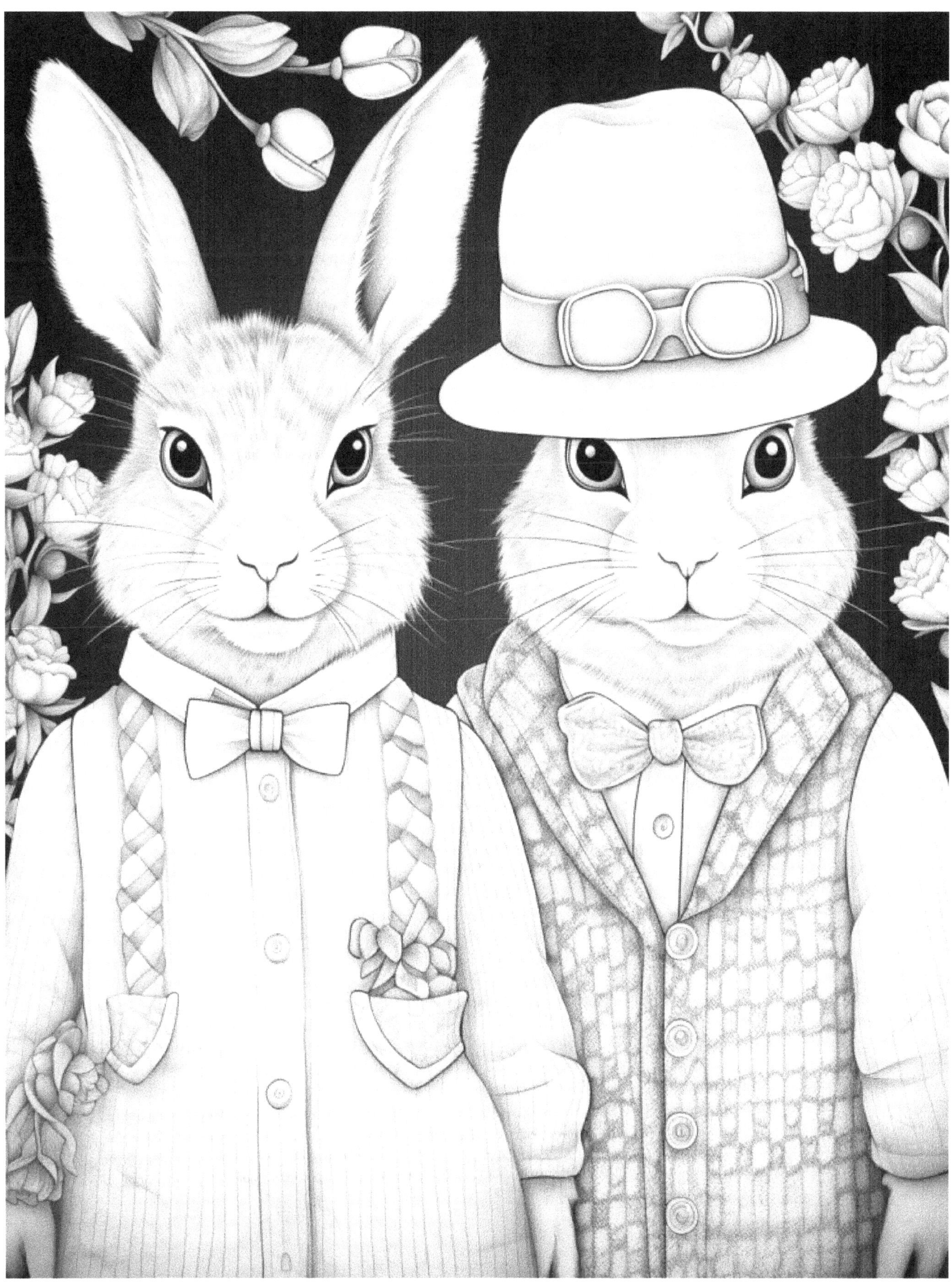

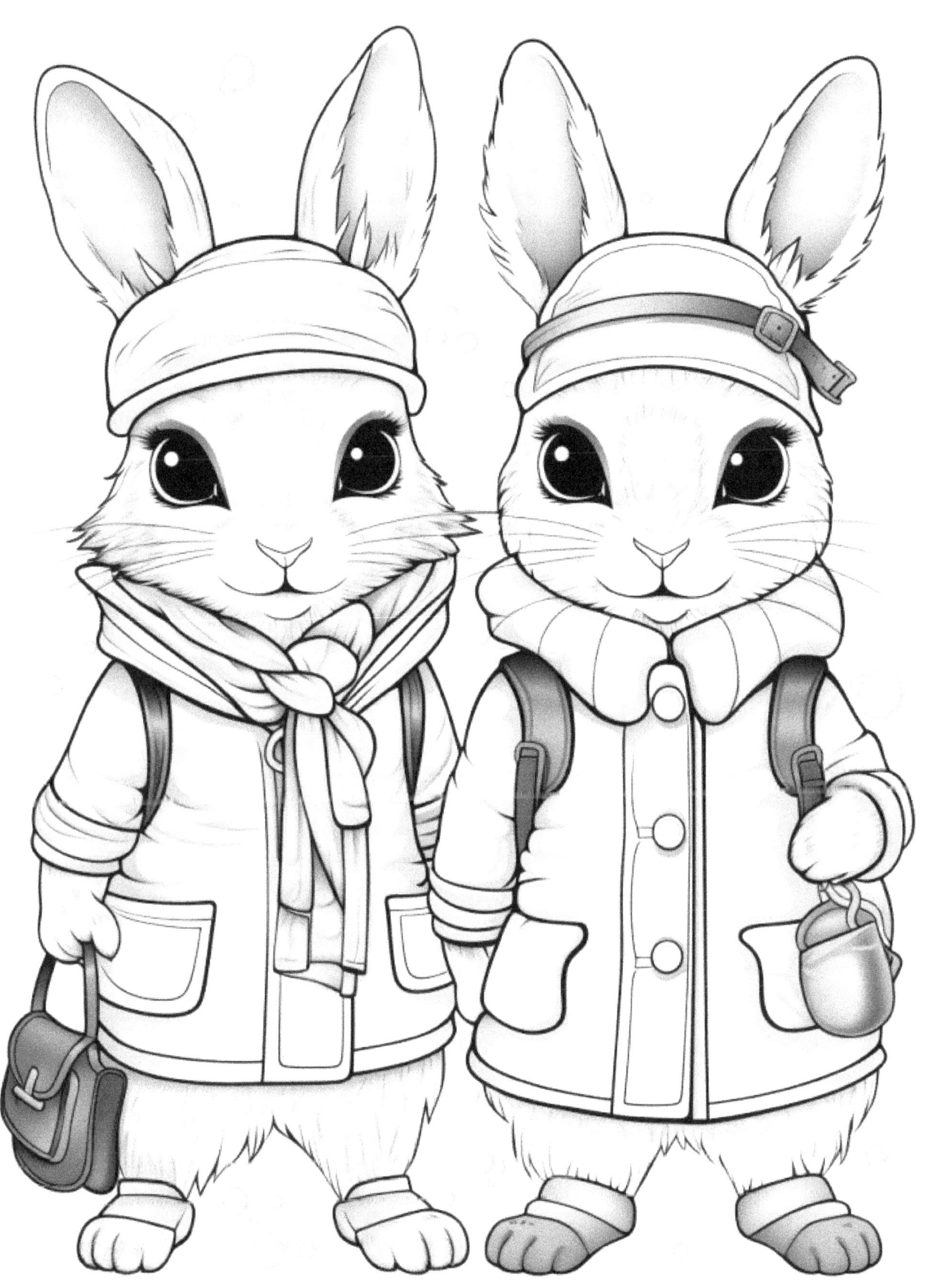

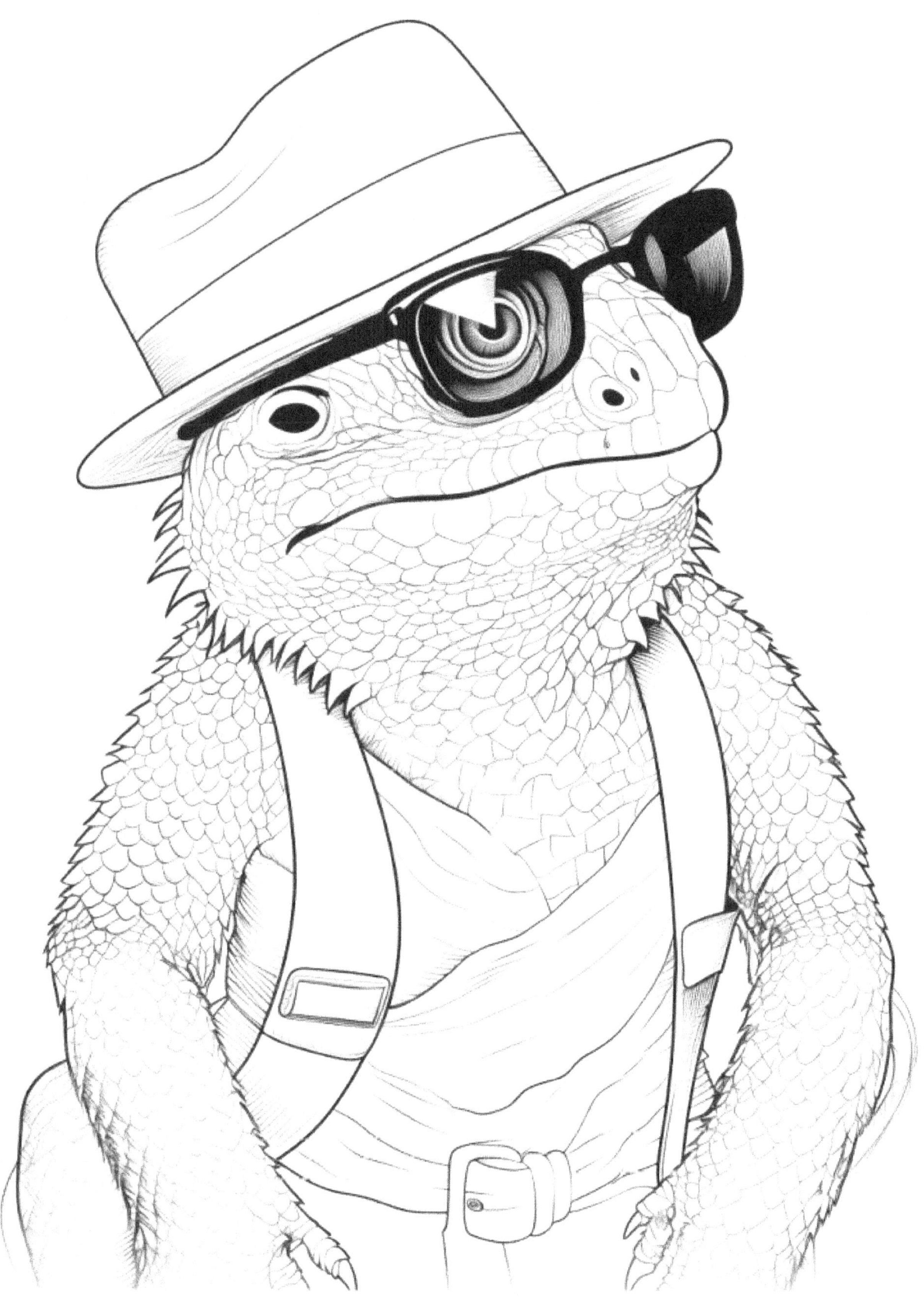

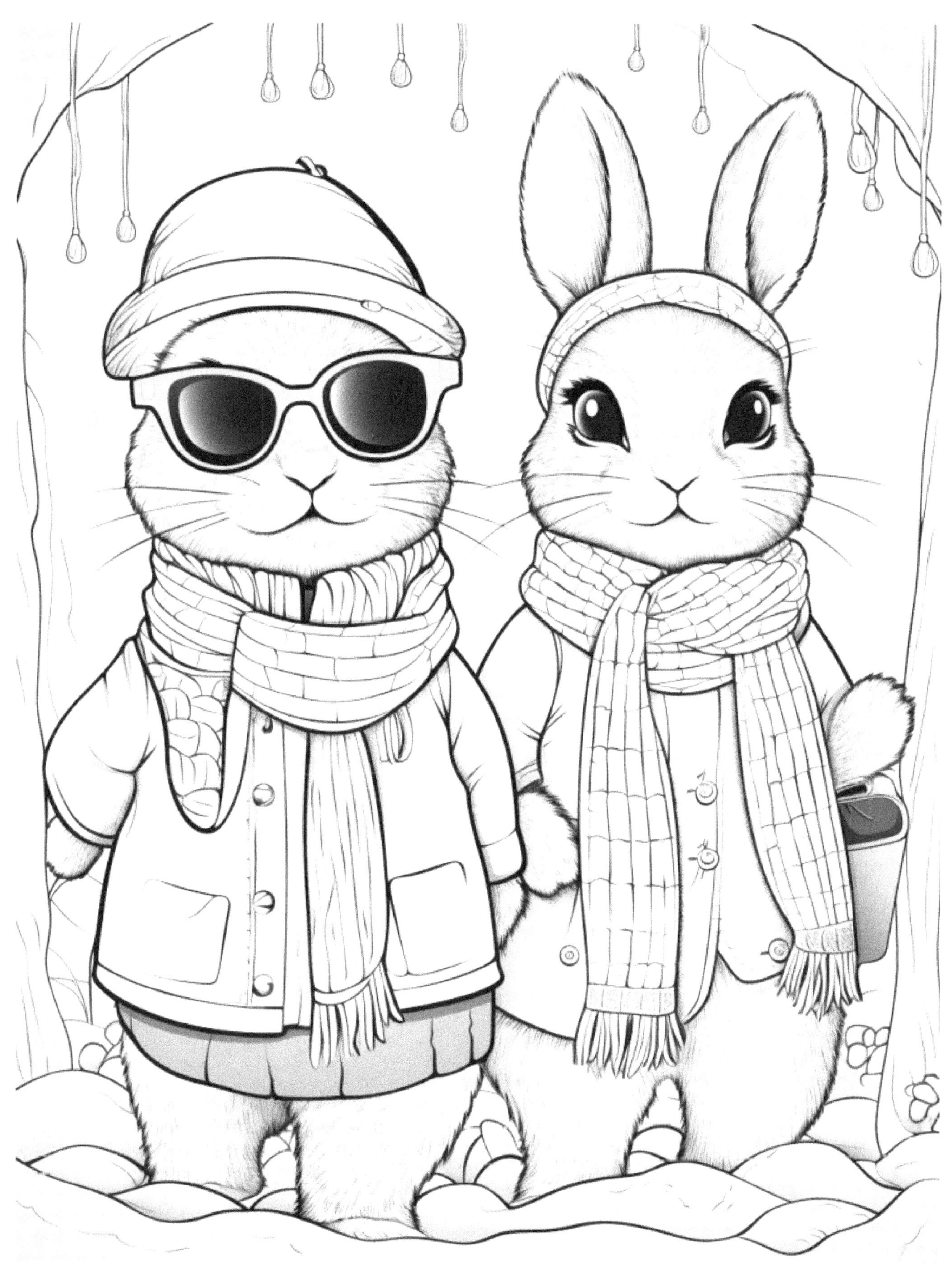

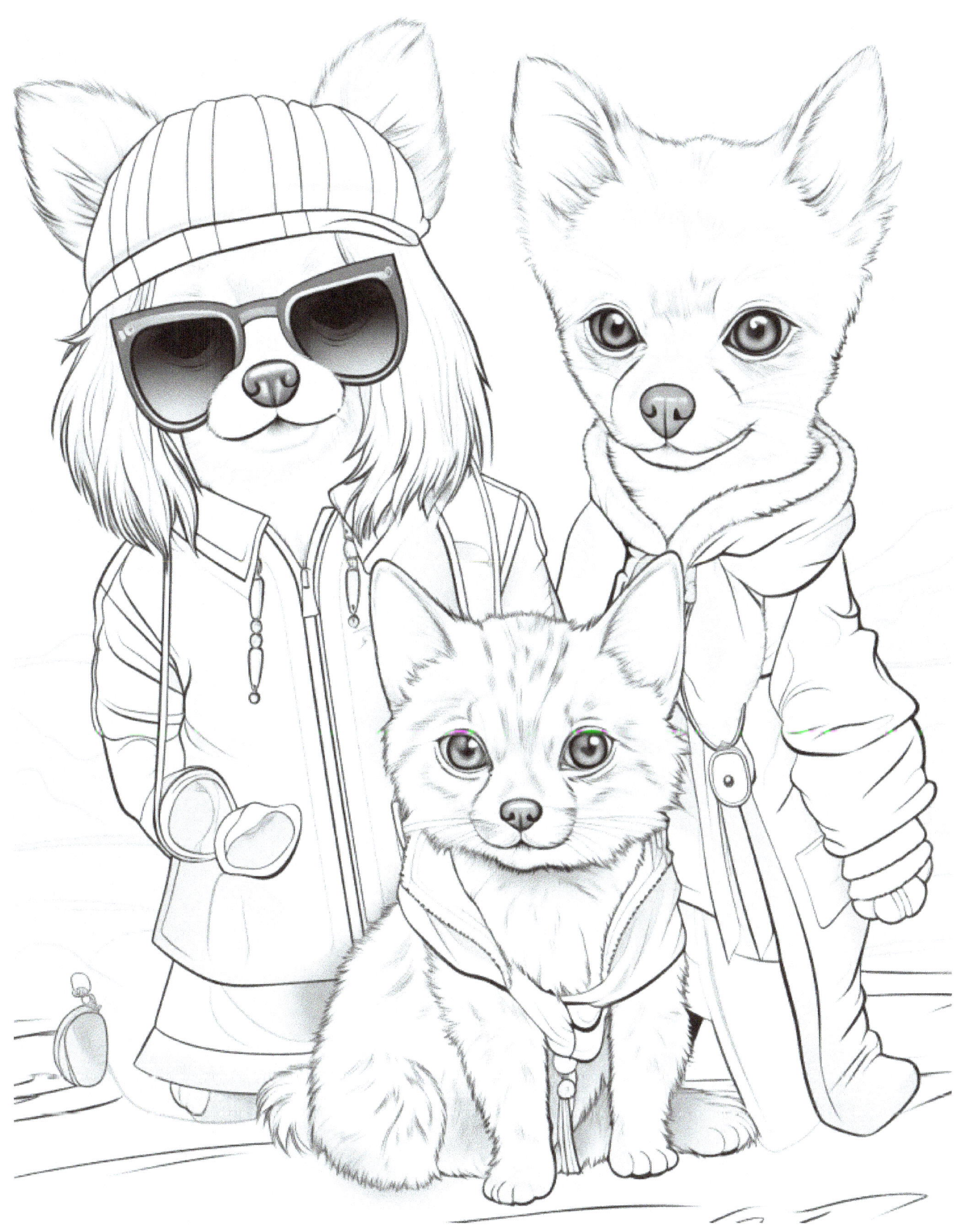

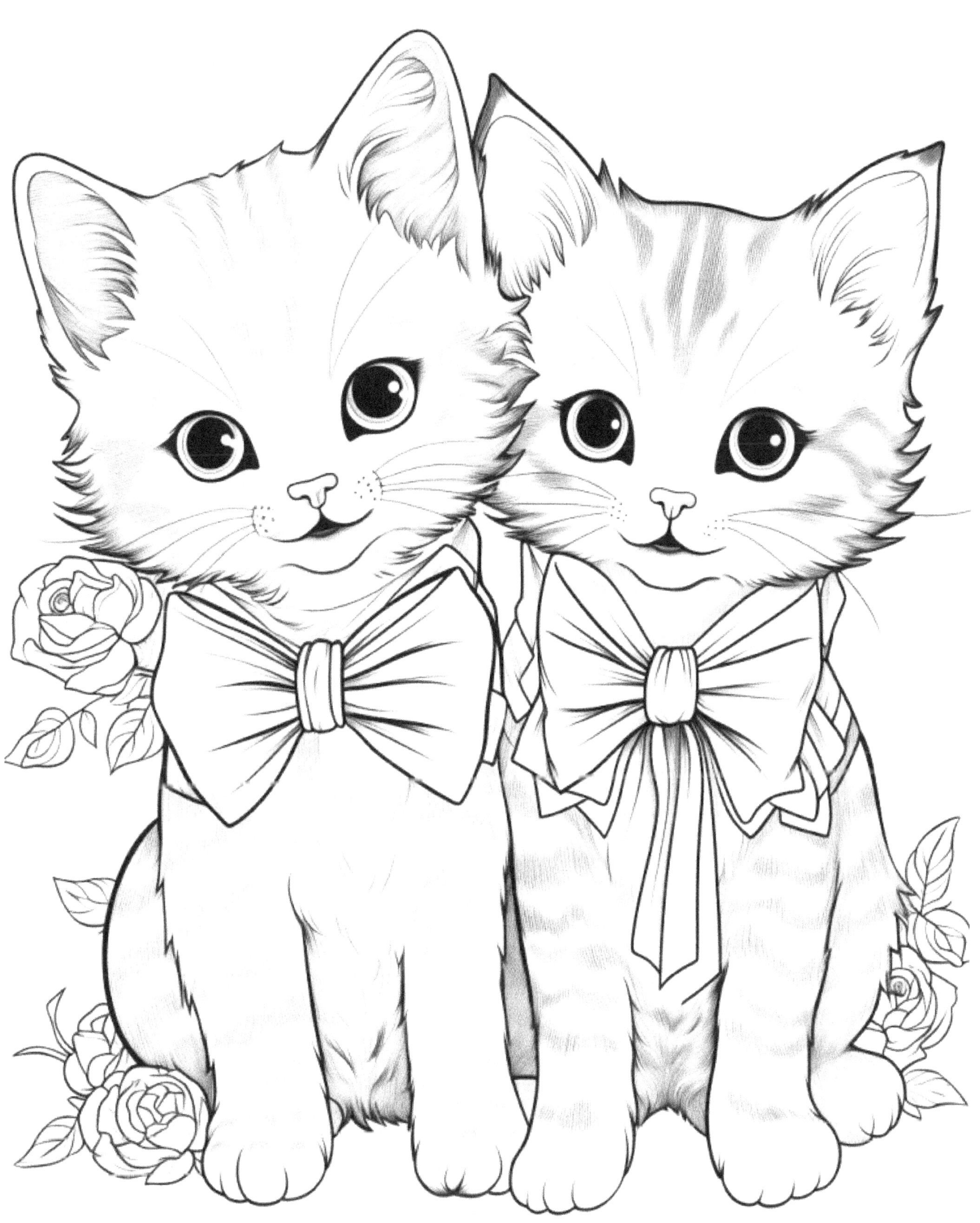

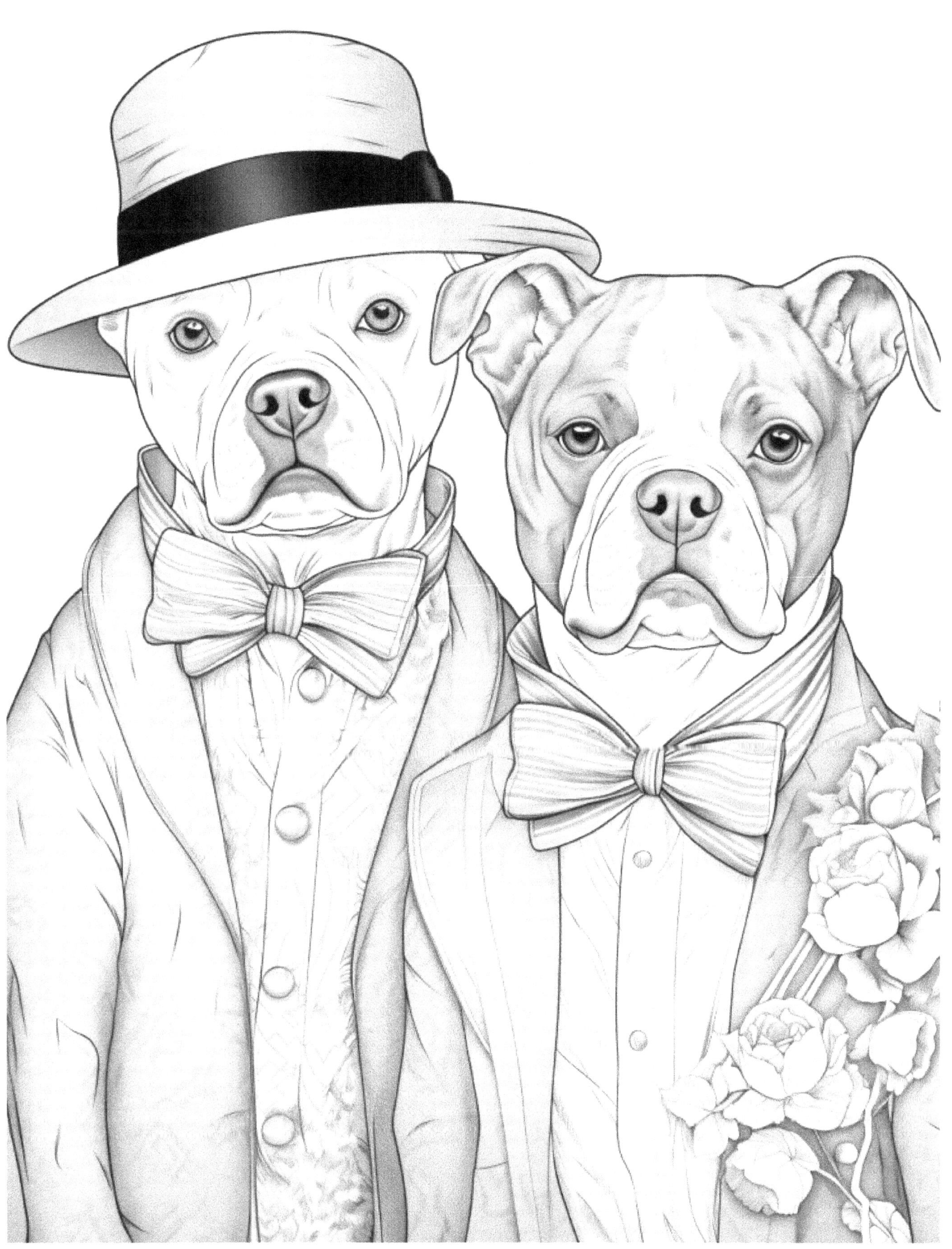

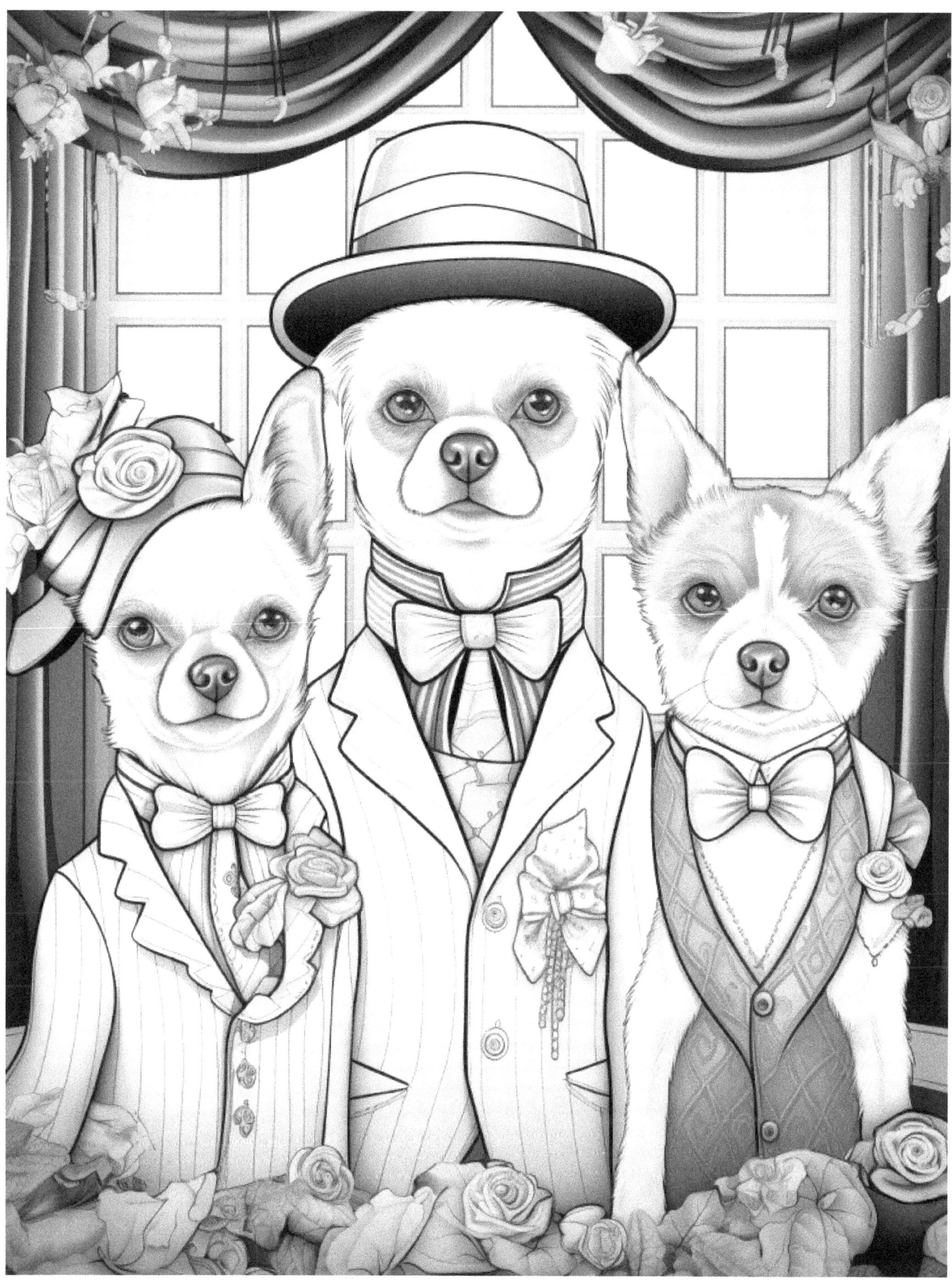

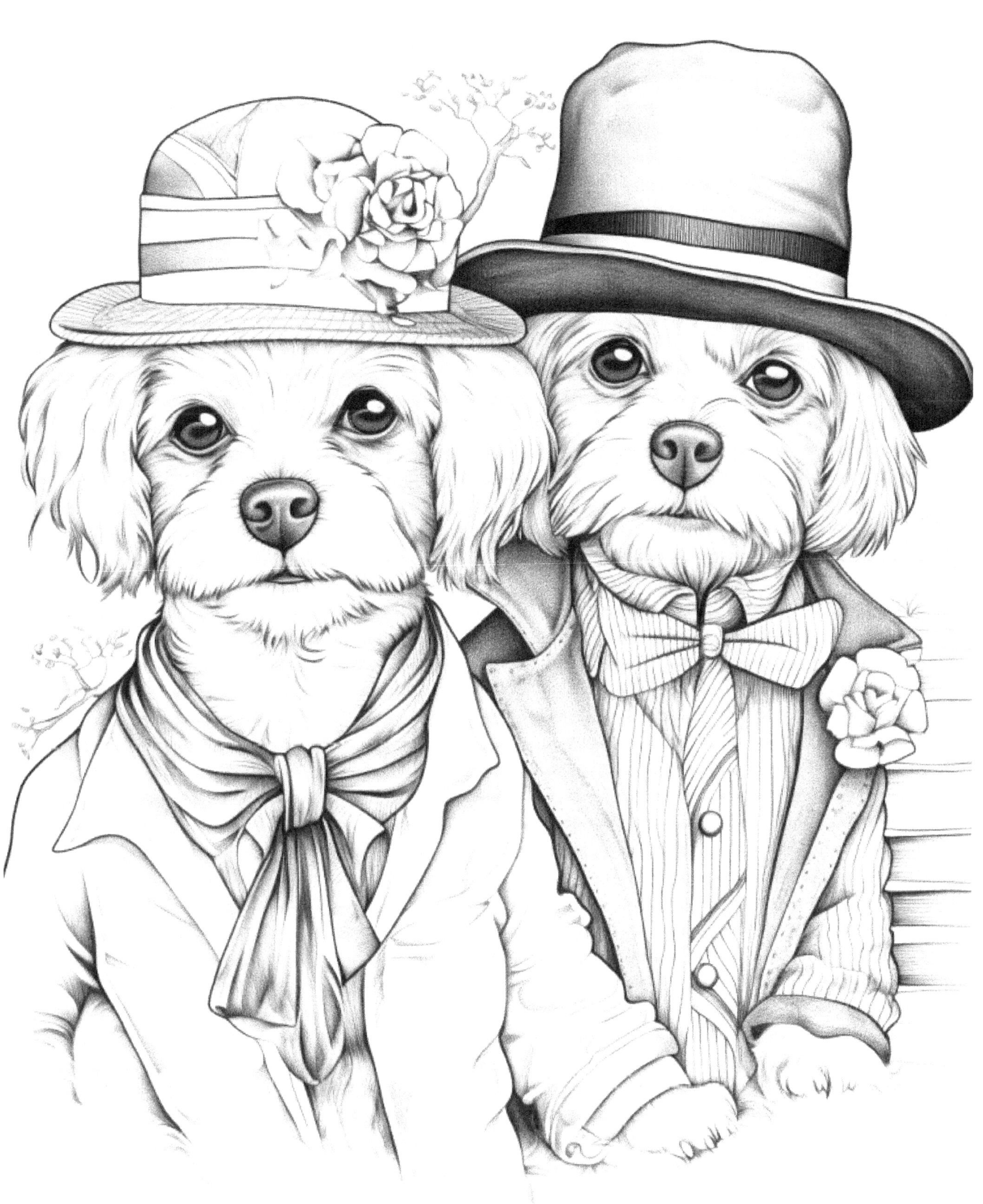

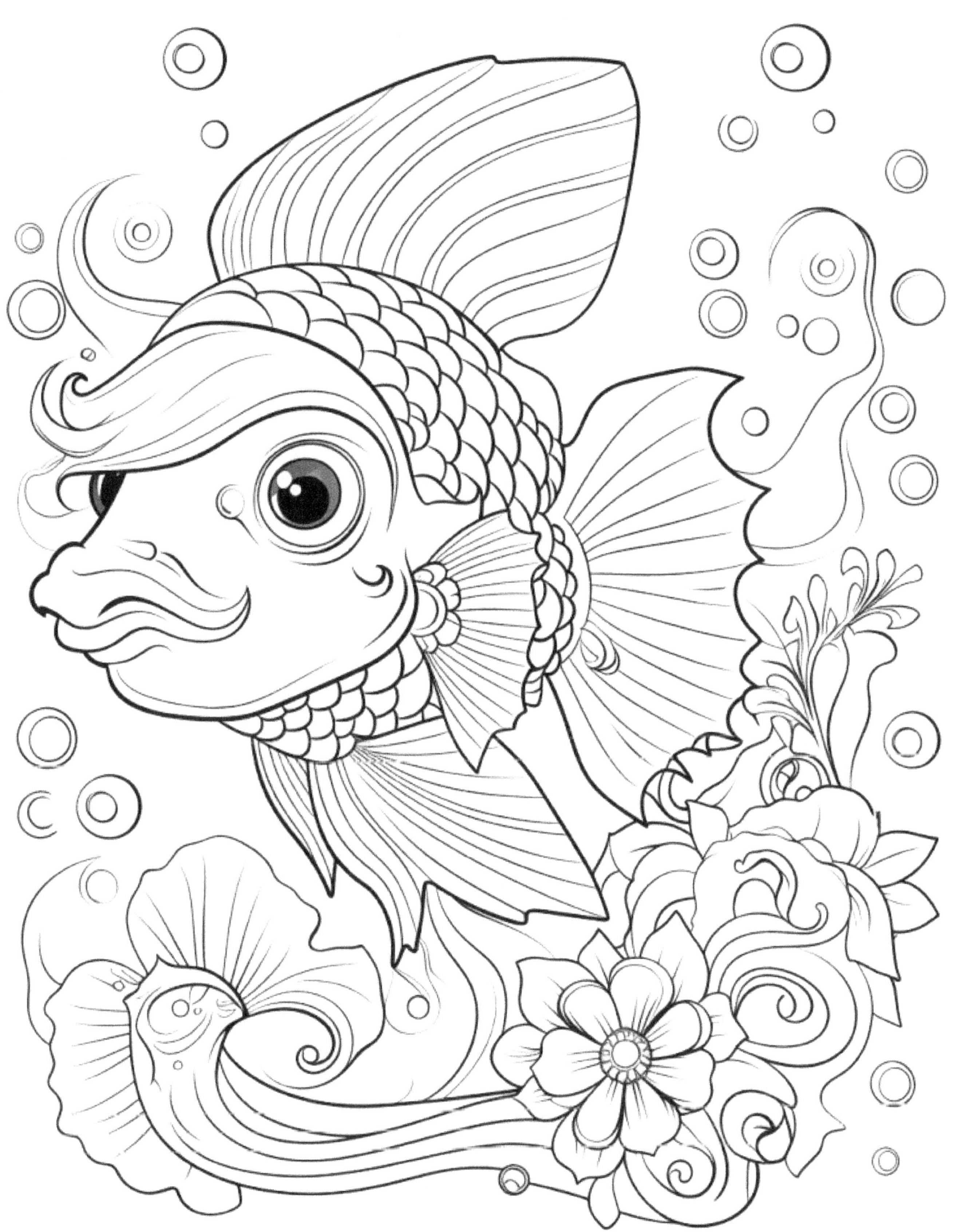

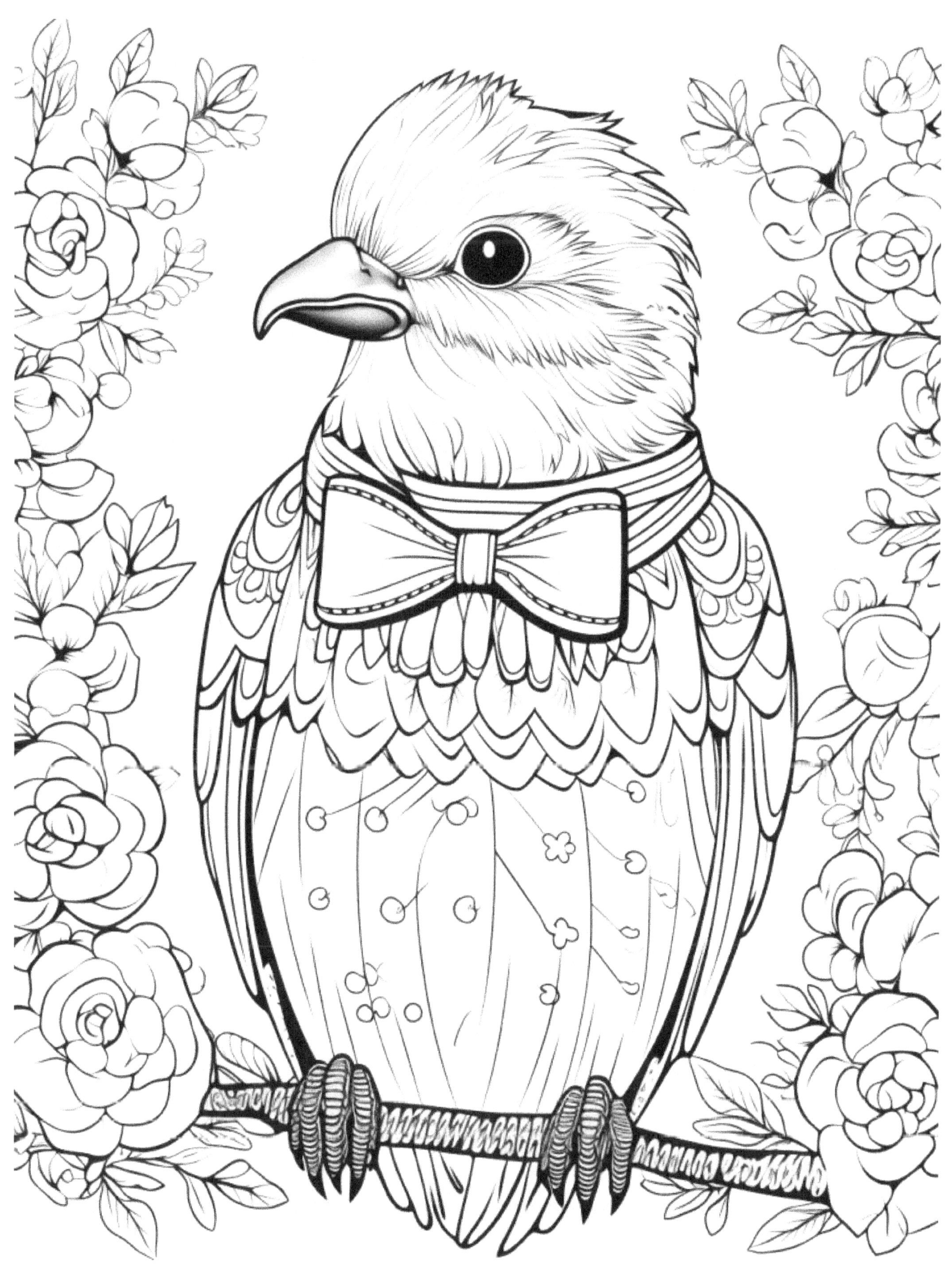

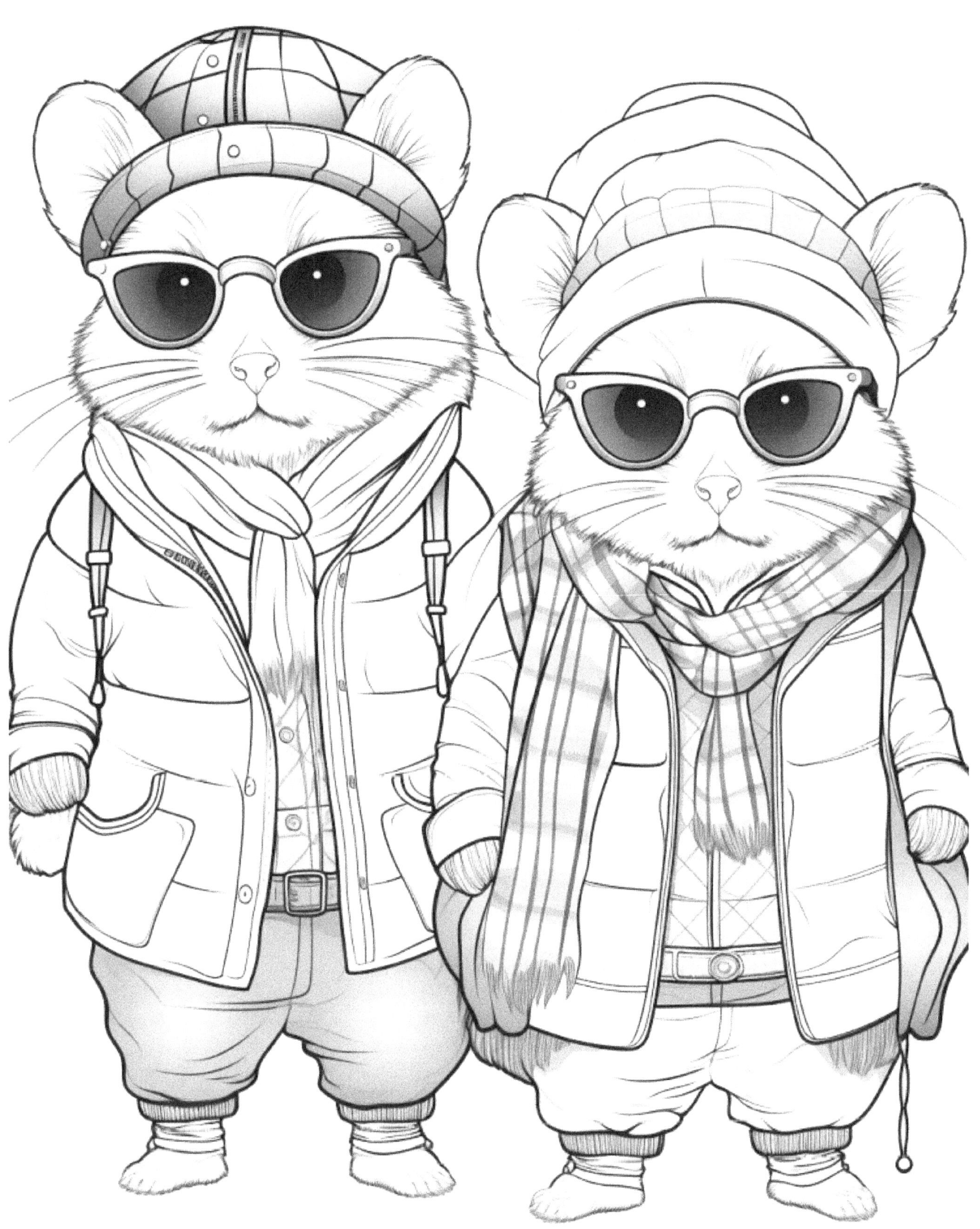

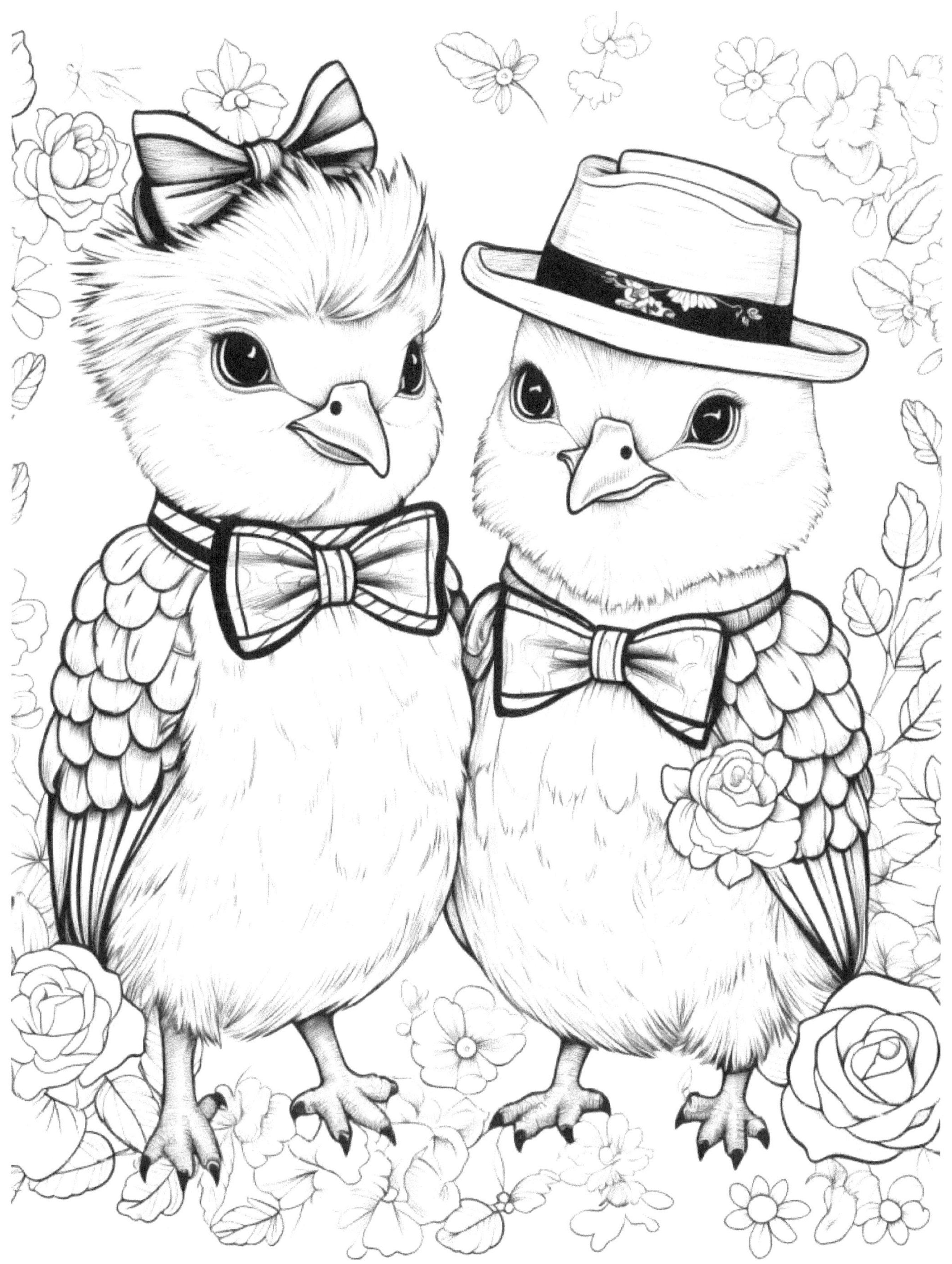

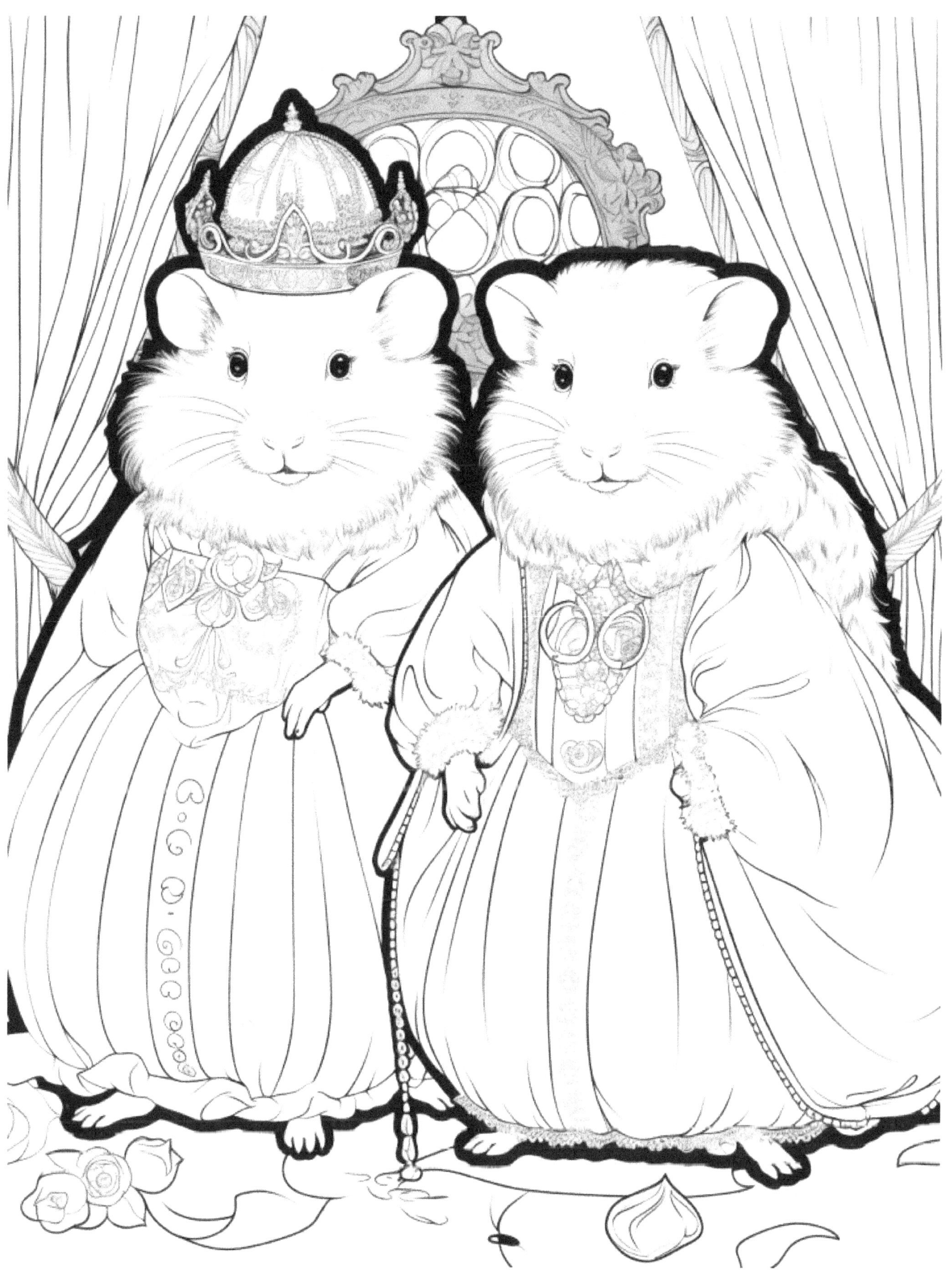

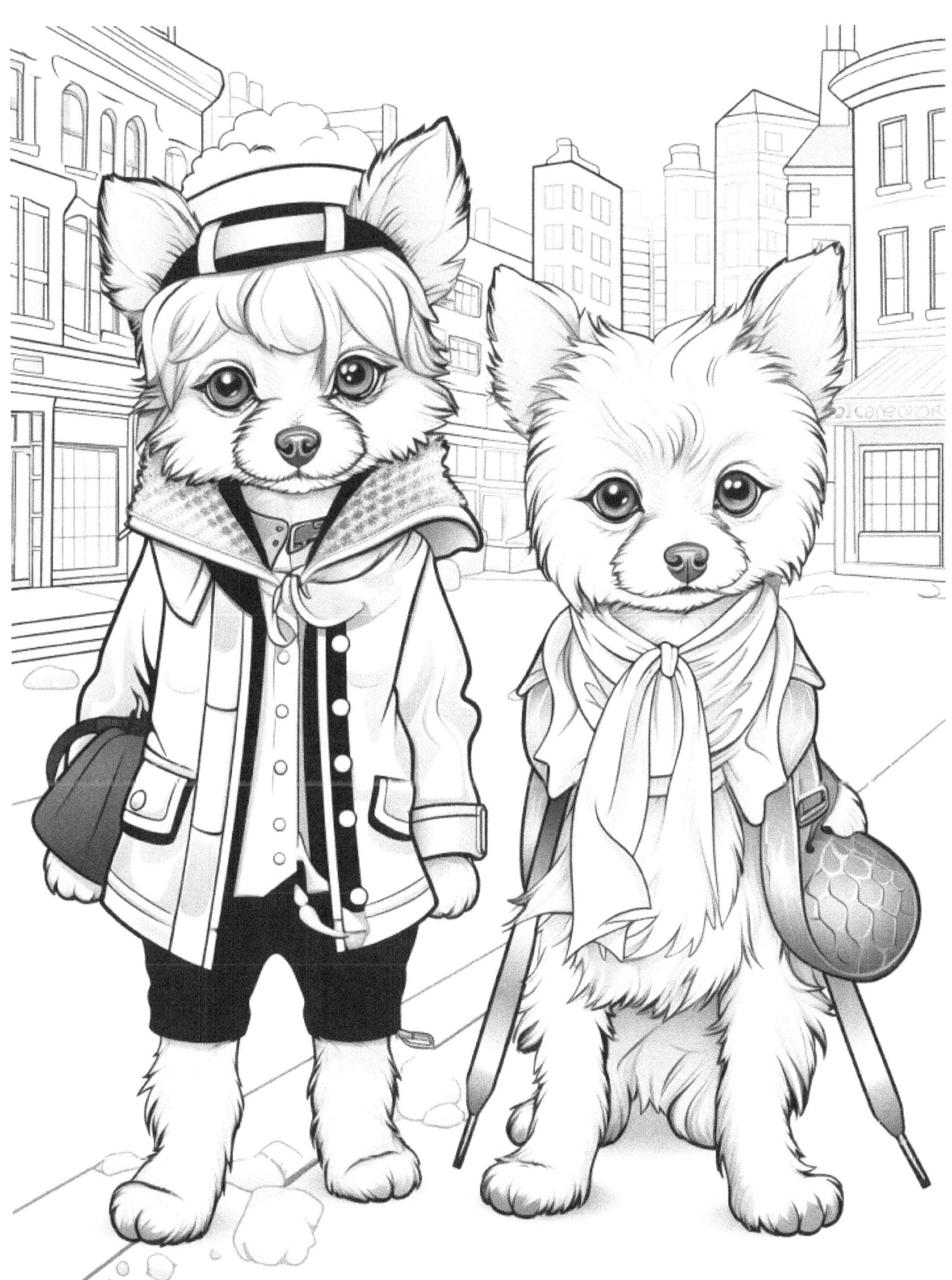

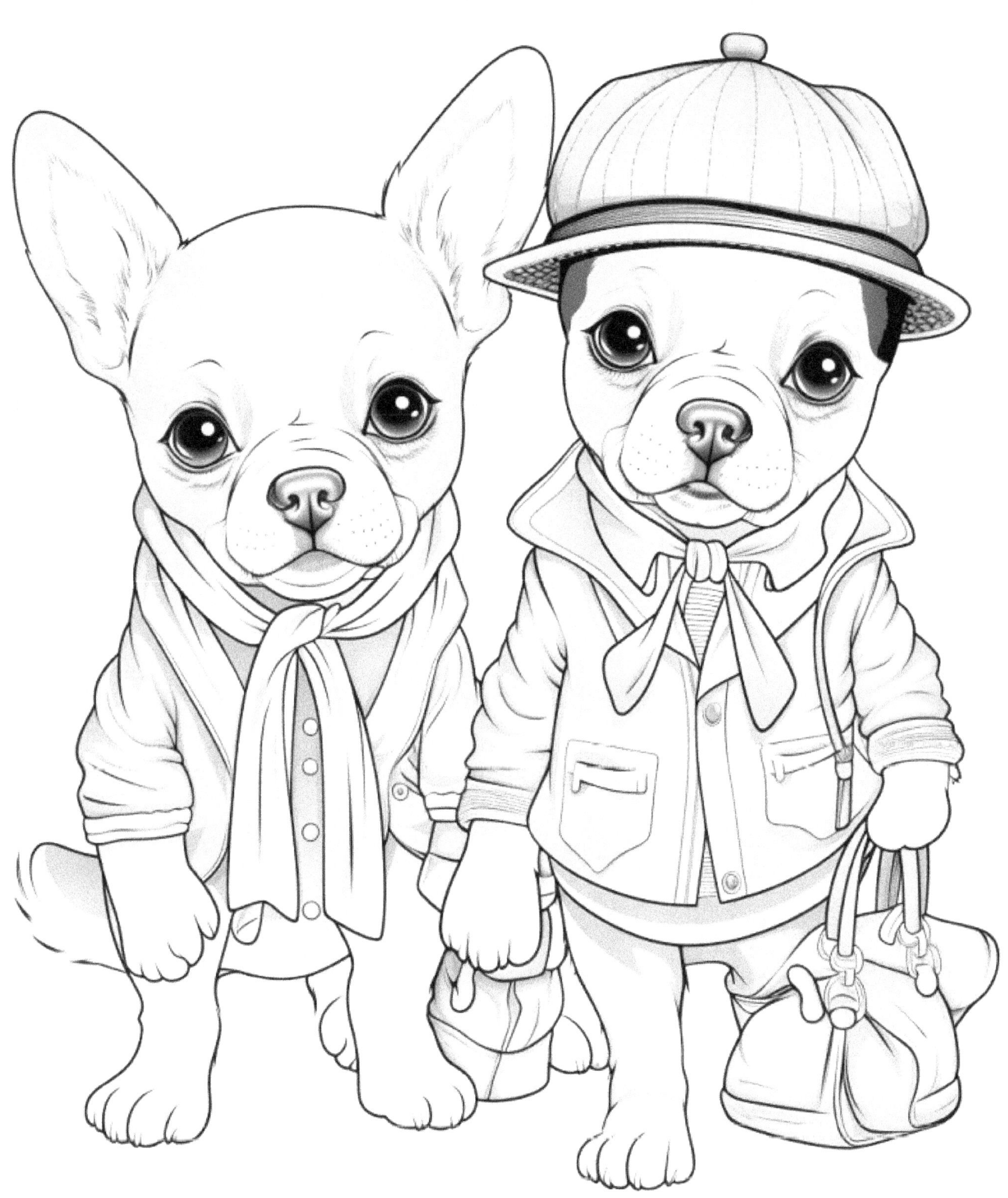

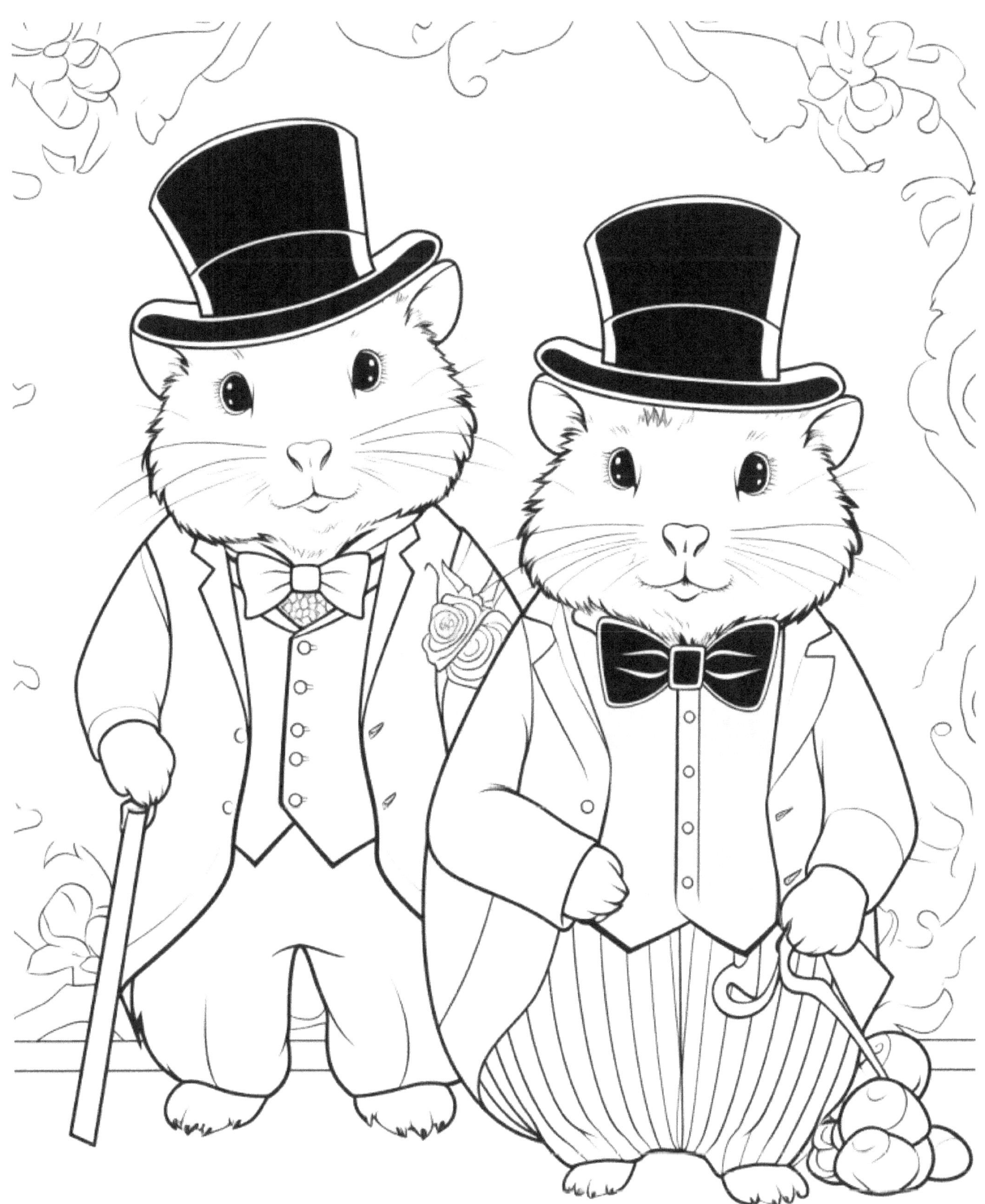

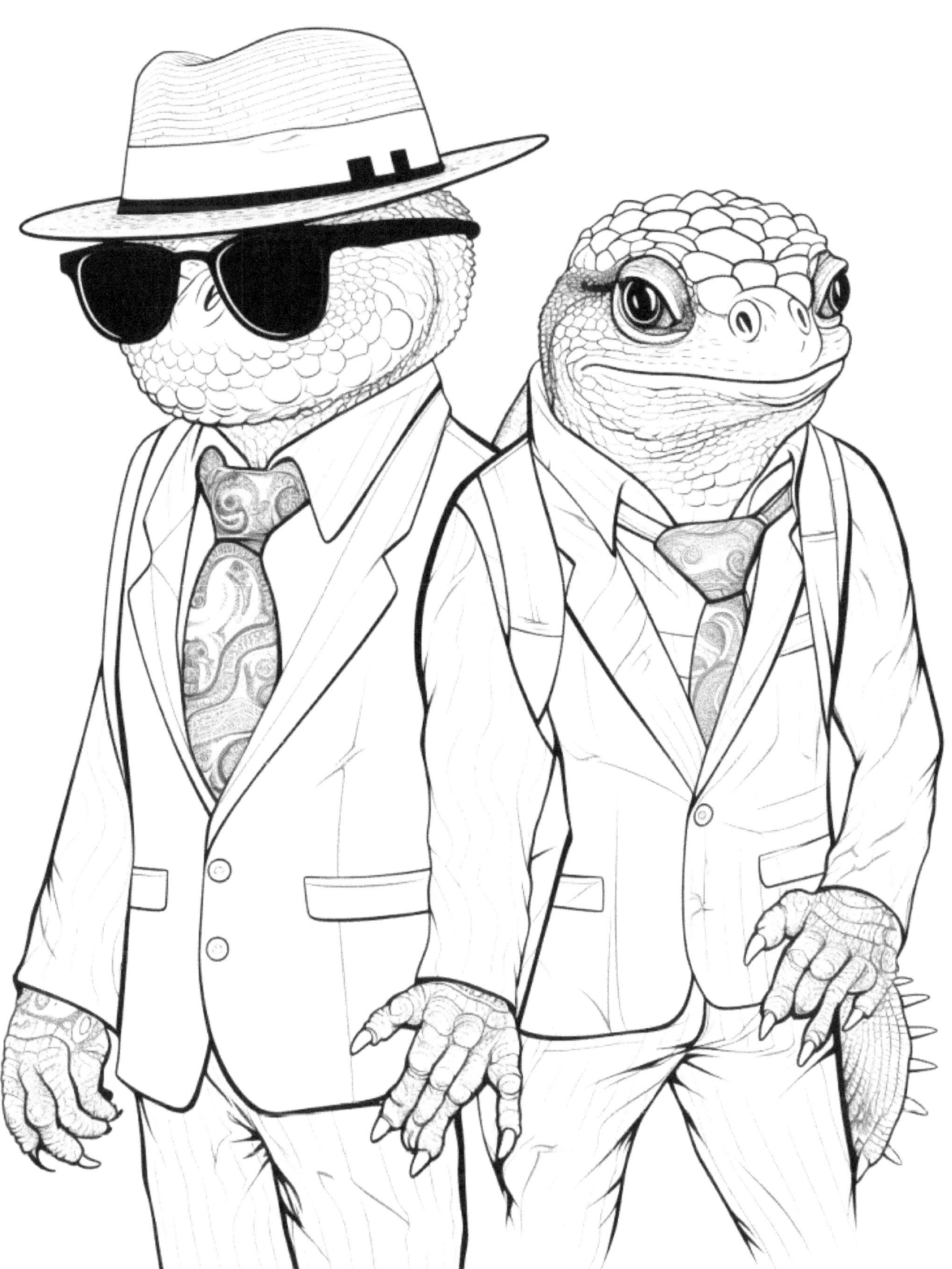

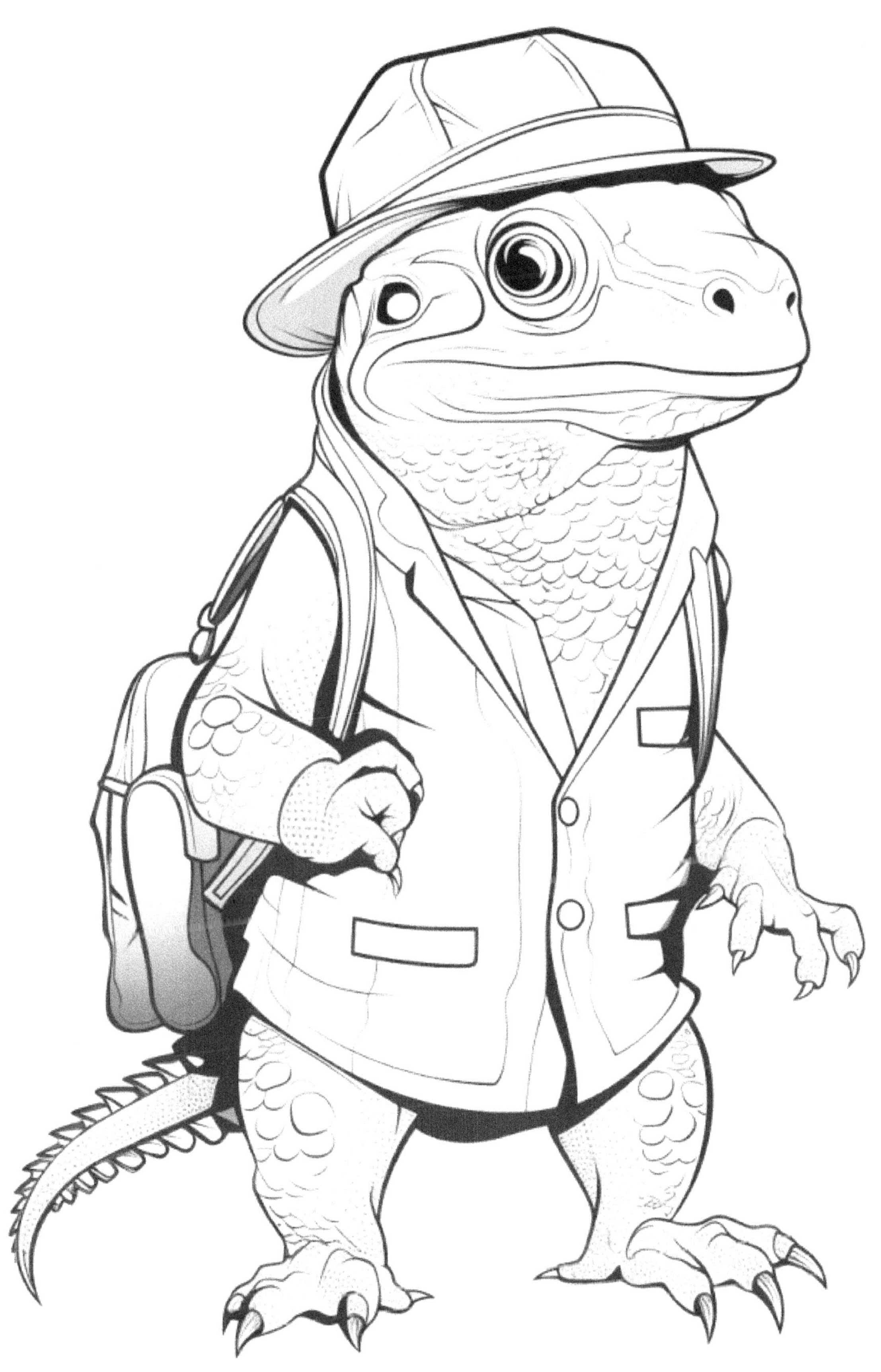

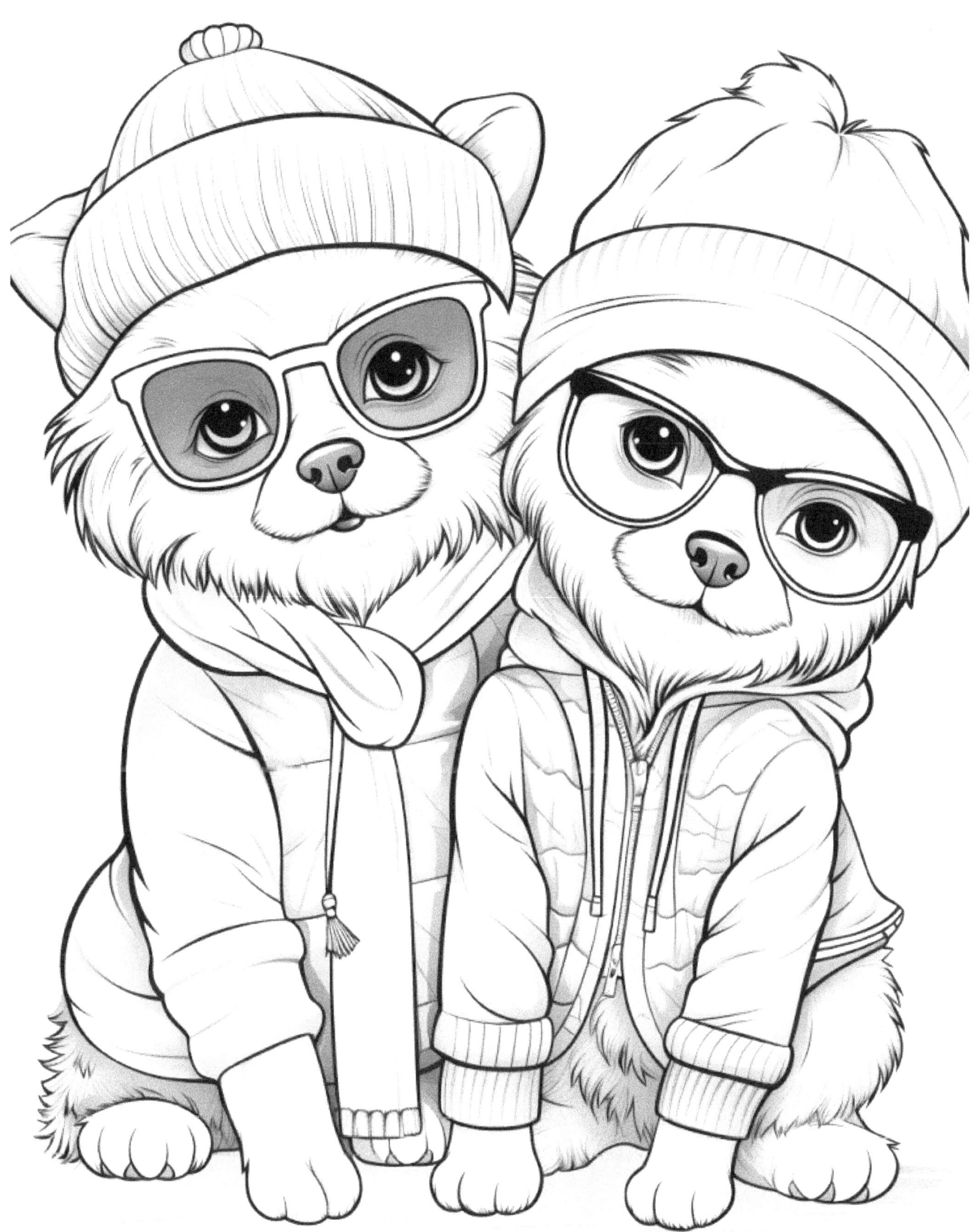

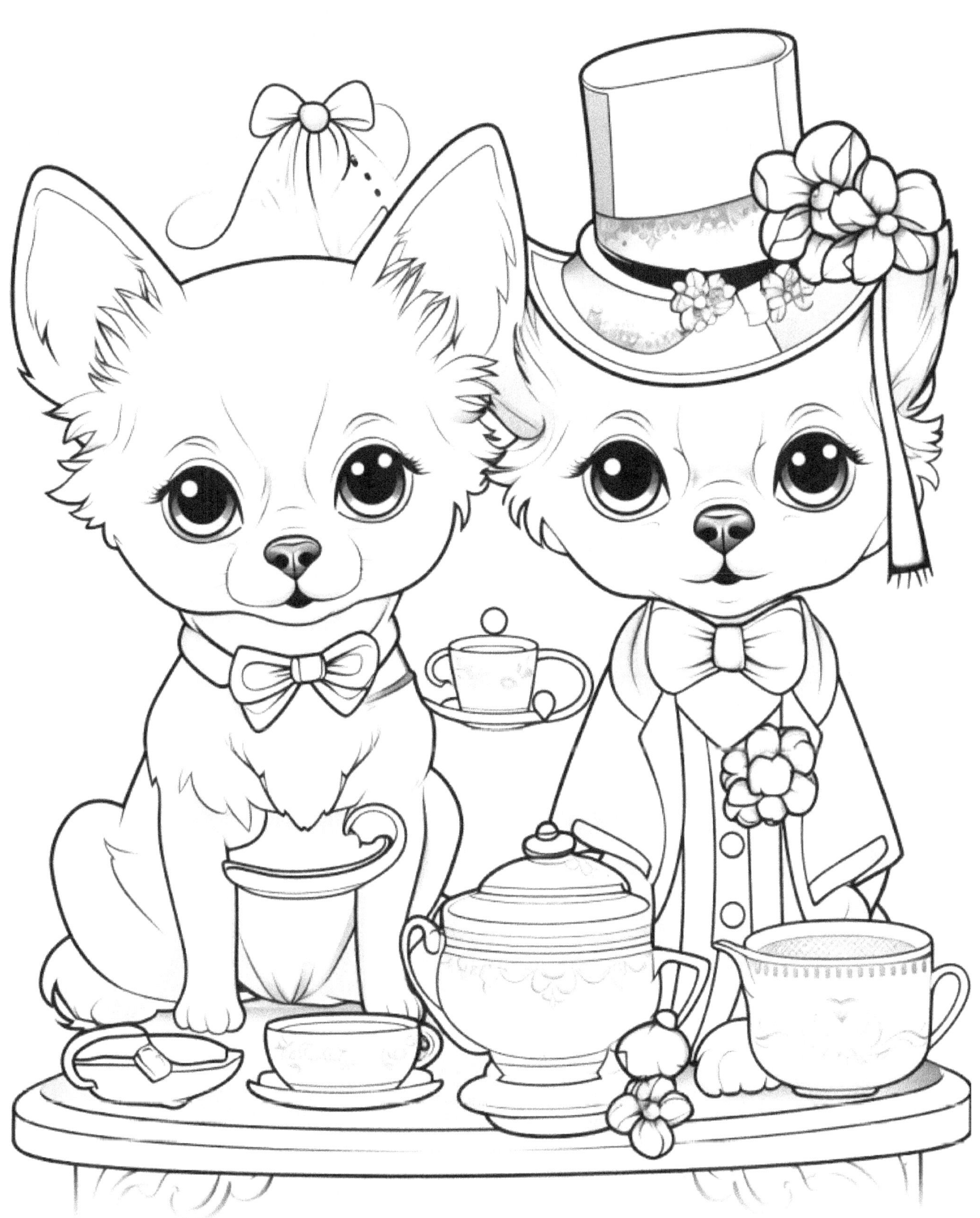

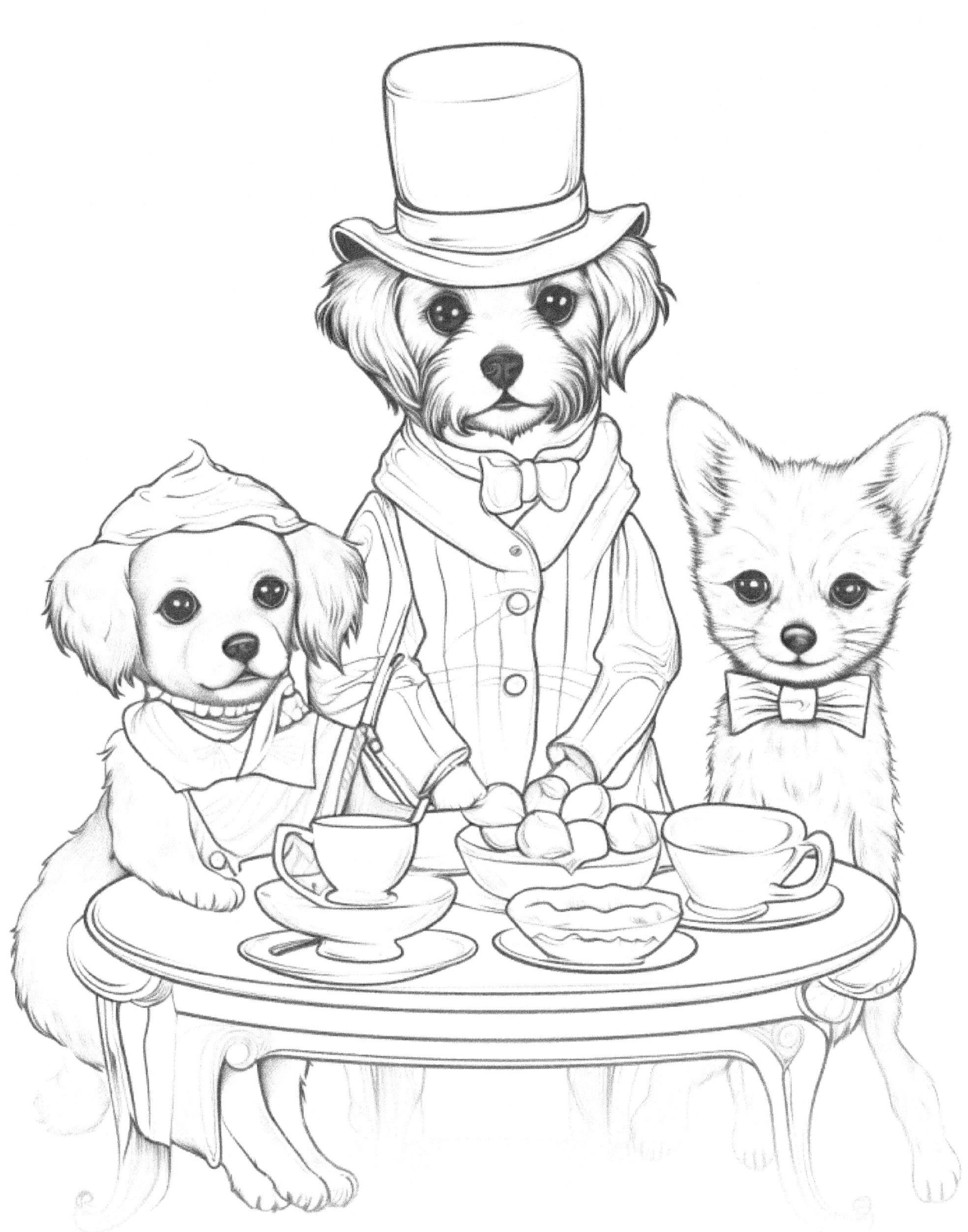

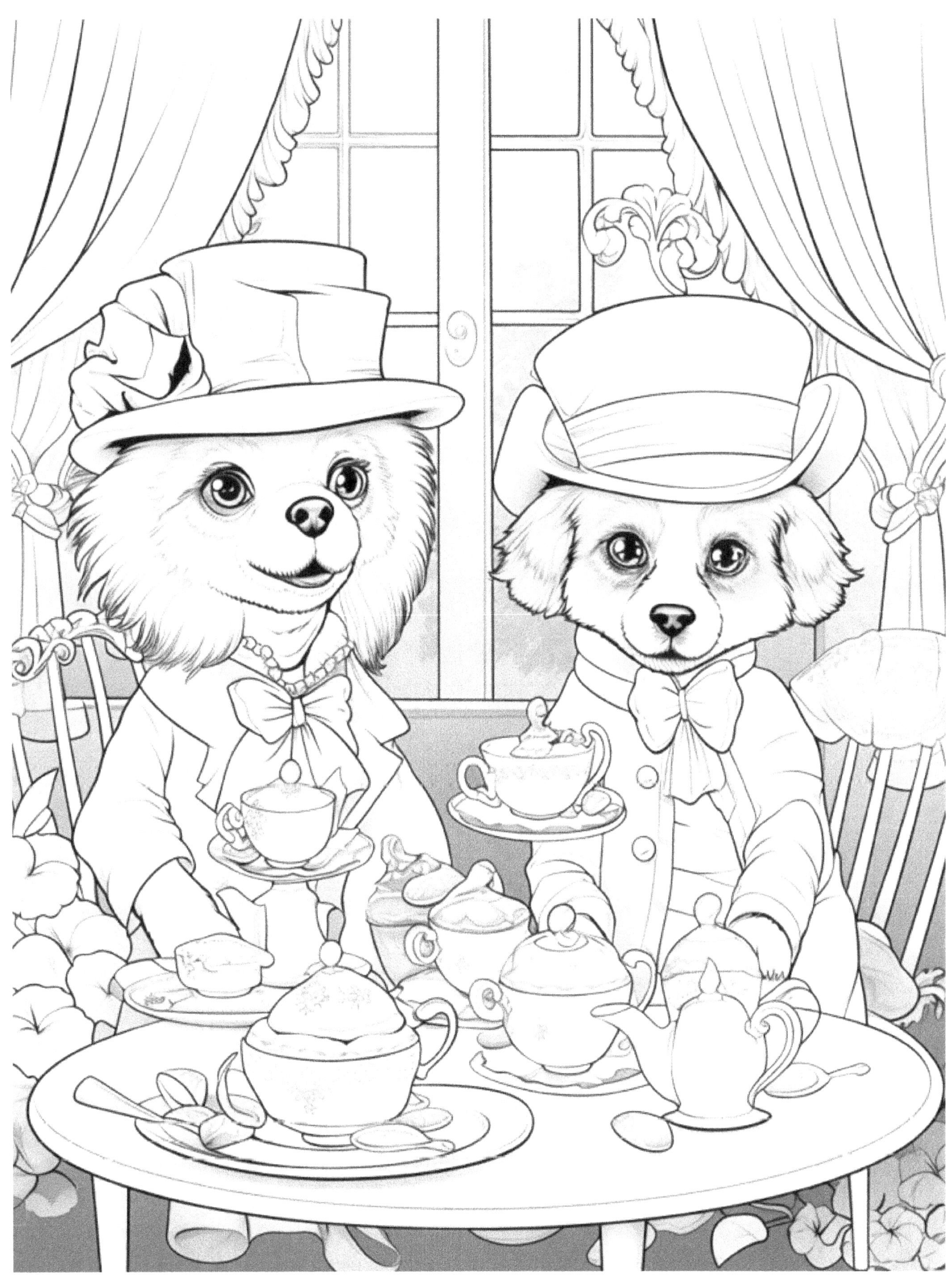

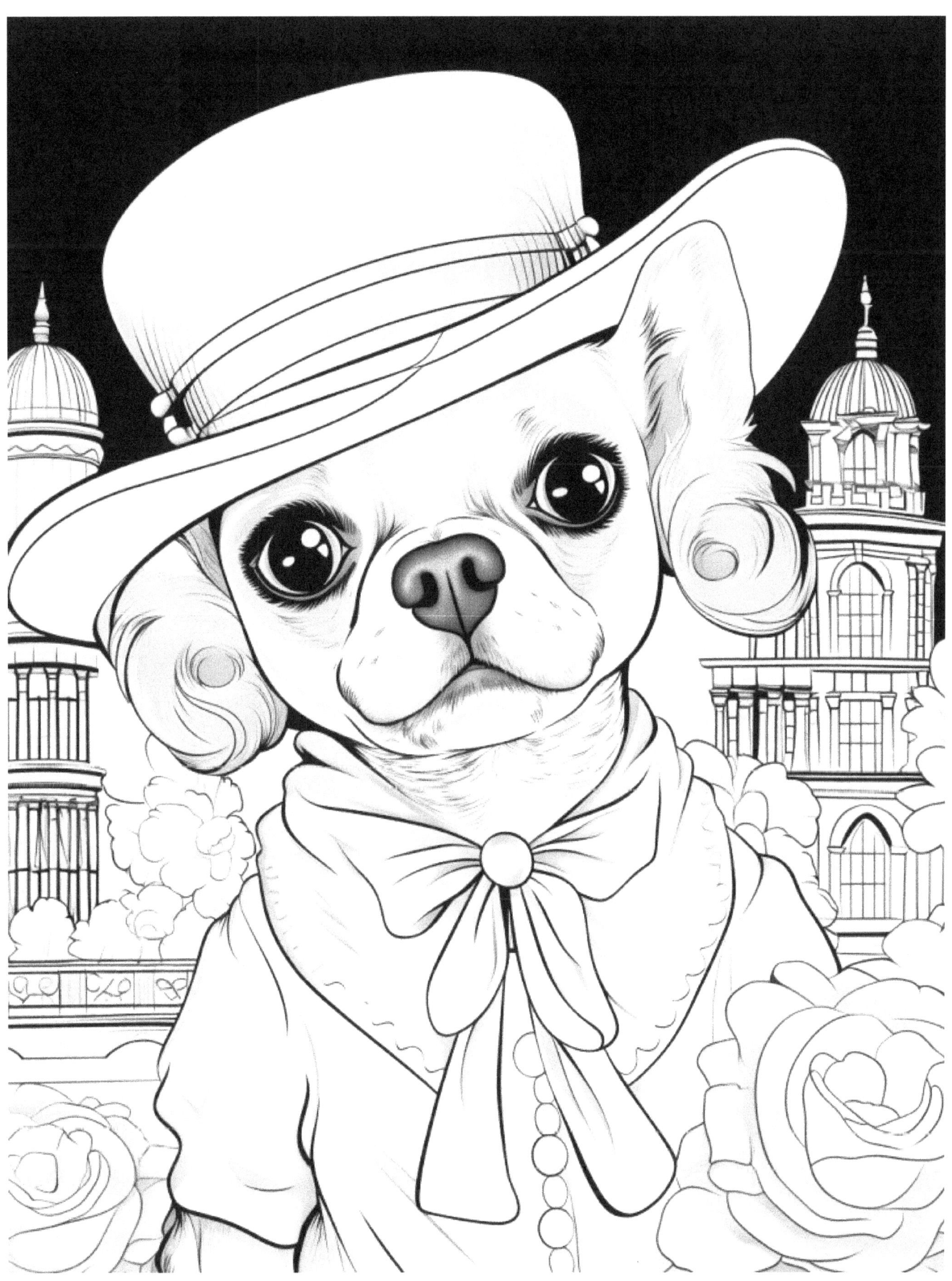